A Mathematicians Miscellany

A MATHEMATICIAN'S MISCELLANY

J. E. LITTLEWOOD

A
Mathematician's
Miscellany

METHUEN & CO. LTD. LONDON
36 *Essex Street, Strand, W.C.* 2

First published in 1953

CATALOGUE NO. 5445/U

PRINTED IN GREAT BRITAIN

ACKNOWLEDGEMENTS

Acknowledgements are due for permission to reprint the following articles and reviews. To the Editor of the *Mathematical Gazette* for ' Newton and the Attraction of a Sphere ', ' Large Numbers ', and the review of Ramanujan's Collected Papers. To the Editor of the *Spectator* and Mr. Arthur Robinson for the Competition Prize Entry, p. 41. To the Editor of the *Cambridge Review* for the batch of three reviews, p. 91.

I have profited by criticisms and suggestions from Dr. T. M. Flett and Mr. J. M. K. Vyvyan. I am under a special debt to Professor T. A. A. Broadbent, who read everything critically : the 'Fermat' article was drastically rewritten in the light of his comments. I am under another special debt to Dr. Flett, who drew the diagrams for me.

CONTENTS

Introduction

§ 1. A Miscellany is a collection without a natural order-
ing relation; I shall not attempt a spurious unity by
imposing artificial ones. I hope that variety may com-
pensate for this lack, except for those irreconcilable persons
who demand an appearance of unity and uniform level.

Anyone open to the idea of looking through a popular
book on mathematics should be able to get on with this one.
I will describe, and sometimes address, him as an ' amateur '.
I constantly meet people who are doubtful, generally without due reason, about their potential capacity. The first
test is whether you got anything out of geometry. To have
disliked or failed to get on with other subjects need mean
nothing ; much drill and drudgery is unavoidable before
they can get started, and bad teaching can make them unintelligible even to a born mathematician. If your education just included, or just stopped short of including, ' a
little calculus ', you are fairly high in the amateur class.

The book contains pieces of technical mathematics, on
occasion pieces that only a professional mathematician can
follow ; these have been included as contributing to the full
picture of the moment as viewed by the professional, but
they can all be skipped without prejudice to the rest, and a
coherent story will remain. I have enclosed between ⋆'s
sections which the amateur should probably skip (but he
need not give up too soon). Outside these I have aimed
consciously at a level to suit his needs (and here it is the
professional who will have to skip at times).

The qualities I have aimed at in selecting material are
two. First relative unfamiliarity, even to some mathematicians. This is why some things receive only bare
mention. They complete a picture (like the technical pieces

above) but are not essential to the amateur (anything that is is given in full). He should on no account be put off if he does not happen to know them (and I generally give references). A specific case happens at the very beginning; (1) of § 2 and the succeeding paragraph. 'Familiar' here means 'familiar to the mathematician'. But experience shows that some amateurs will know Euclid's proof; if so, they will also know that it is so familiar that I must not discuss it [1]; it shows on the other hand that some do not know it; it is they who must not be put off.

The other quality is lightness, notwithstanding the highbrow pieces; my aim is entertainment and there will be no uplift. I must leave this to the judgment of my readers, but I shall have failed where they find anything cheap or trivial. A good mathematical joke is better, and better mathematics, than a dozen mediocre papers.

[1] There is, however, a 1-line indication for the professional on p. 20.

Mathematics with minimum 'raw material'

§ 2. What pieces of genuine mathematics come under this ? A *sine qua non* is certainly that the *result* should be intelligible to the amateur. We need not insist that the *proof* also should (see e.g. examples (15), (16), (19)), though most often it is. I begin with clear cases ; later on we shade off and the latest examples are there because for various reasons they happen to appeal to my particular taste. Various things that belong to a complete picture are ' mentioned ' or postponed.

(1) Euclid's ('familiar') proof that the primes are infinite in number is obviously in the running for the highest place. (See e.g. Hardy's *A Mathematician's Apology*, pp. 32-34, or p. 20 below.)

The ' familiar ' things in § 4 belong here ; but to make them intelligible to the amateur would call for interrupting explanation.

My actual choice for first place is a well-known puzzle that swept Europe a good many years ago and in one form or another has appeared in a number of books. I revert to the original form, in which A's flash of insight is accounted for by an emotional stimulus.

(2) Three ladies, A, B, C in a railway carriage all have dirty faces and are all laughing. It suddenly flashes on A : why doesn't B realize C is laughing at her ?—Heavens ! *I* must be laughable. (Formally : if I, A, am not laughable, B will be arguing : if I, B, am not laughable, C has nothing to laugh at. Since B does not so argue, I, A, must be laughable.)

This is genuine mathematical reasoning, and surely with

3

minimum material. But further, what has not got into the
books so far as I know, there is an extension, in principle,
to n ladies, all dirty and all laughing. There is an induction :
in the $(n+1)$-situation A argues : if I am not laughable,
B, C, . . . constitute an n-situation and B would stop
laughing, but does not.

Compare the rule for toasting 3 slices of bread on a
toaster that holds only 2. A_1, B_1 ; then B_2, C_1 ; then C_2,
A_2. This falls short of being mathematics.

(3) The following will probably not stand up to close
analysis, but given a little goodwill is entertaining.

There is an indefinite supply of cards marked 1 and 2 on
opposite sides, and of cards marked 2 and 3, 3 and 4, and
so on. A card is drawn at random by a referee and held
between the players A, B so that each sees one side only.
Either player may veto the round, but if it is played the
player seeing the higher number wins. The point now is
that every round is vetoed. If A sees a 1 the other side is
2 and he must veto. If he sees a 2 the other side is 1 or 3 ;
if 1 then B must veto ; if he does not then A must. And
so on by induction.

(4) An analogous example (Schrödinger) is as follows.
We have cards similar to those in (3), but this time there are
10^n of the ones of type $(n, n+1)$, and the player seeing the
lower number wins. A and B may now bet each with a
bookie (or for that matter with each other), backing themselves at evens. The position now is that whatever A sees
he ' should ' bet, and the same is true of B, the odds in
favour being 9 to 1. Once the monstrous hypothesis has
been got across (as it generally has), then, whatever number
n A sees, it is 10 times more probable that the other side is
$n+1$ than that it is $n-1$. (Incidentally, whatever number
N is assigned before a card is drawn, it is infinitely probable
that the numbers on the card will be greater than N.)

(5) *An infinity paradox.* Balls numbered 1, 2, ... (or for a mathematician the numbers themselves) are put into a box as follows. At 1 minute to noon the numbers 1 to 10 are put in, and the number 1 is taken out. At $\frac{1}{2}$ minute to noon numbers 11 to 20 are put in and the number 2 is taken out. At $\frac{1}{3}$ minute 21 to 30 in and 3 out ; and so on. How many are in the box at noon ? The answer is none : any selected number, e.g. 100, is absent, having been taken out at the 100th operation.

★ An analyst is constantly meeting just such things ; confronted with the set of points

$$P_1+P_2+\cdots+P_{10}-P_1+P_{11}+\cdots+P_{20}-P_2+\cdots,$$

he would at once observe that it was ' null ', and without noticing anything paradoxical.★

On the subject of paradoxes I will digress into Celestial Mechanics. Suppose n bodies, to be treated as points, are moving subject to the Newtonian law of gravitation. Those systems are infinitely rare [1] for which, sooner or later, a simple collision (collision of two point-bodies only) occurs. It is as certain as anything can be that the same holds for multiple collisions (of three or more point-bodies). (Indeed, while simple collisions are normal for e.g. the inverse cube law, multiple ones are doubtless infinitely rare whatever the law.) Nevertheless there is no proof.

This is of course a paradox about proofs, not about facts. It is also possible to explain it. With simple collisions the analytic character of the behaviour of the system, suitably generalized, survives a simple collision, and it can consequently be seen that a simple collision (at no matter how late a date) involves two analytic relations between the initial conditions, and this makes those conditions infinitely rare.

---

[1] In technical language the set of 'representative points ' (in a space for representing initial conditions) of systems that suffer simple conditions has measure 0.

§ 3. (6) 4 ships A, B, C, D are sailing in a fog with constant and different speeds and constant and different courses. The 5 pairs A and B, B and C, C and A, B and D, C and D have each had near collisions ; call them ' collisions '. Most people find unexpected the mathematical consequence that A and D necessarily ' collide '. Consider the 3-dimensional graphs of position against time—' world lines '—with the axis of time vertical. The world lines a, b, c meet each other ; consequently a, b, c are all in the same one plane, p say ; d meets b and c, so it lies in p, and therefore meets a. (Limiting cases of parallelism are ruled out by the speeds being different.)

(7) *An experiment to prove the rotation of the earth.* A glass tube in the form of an anchor ring is filled with water and rests horizontally, for simplicity at the North Pole. The tube is suddenly rotated through 180° about a horizontal axis. The water is now flowing round the tube (at the rate of a revolution in 12 hours) and the movement can be detected. This might have been invented by Archimedes, but had to wait till 1930 (A. H. Compton). (It is curious how very late many of the things in my collection are. For a change the date of the next one is 1605.)

(8) *Stevinus and gravity on an inclined plane.* A chain $ABCD$, hanging as in Fig. 1, *can* rest in equilibrium (else perpetual motion). The symmetrical lower part ADC exerts equal pulls on AB, BC, and may be removed, leaving ABC in equilibrium. That AB, BC balance is in effect the sine law. (For an interesting discussion see Mach, *Science of Mechanics*, 24-31.)

(9) To determine the orbit of a planet or comet 3 observations, each of two (angular) co-ordinates and the time t, suffice. It is actually the case that to *any* set of observations (point the telescope anyhow at any 3 times) an orbit [1]

---

[1] A conic with the sun as focus.

corresponds. Imagine a speck on the telescope's object glass ; this satisfies the observations, and it also describes an orbit (that of the earth). Now (some sordid details being taken for granted) the equations for the elements of the orbit are reducible to the solution of an equation of the 8th

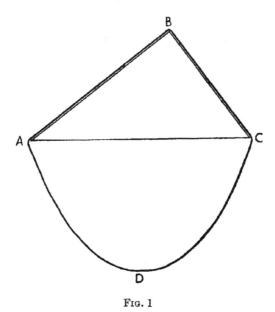

Fig. 1

degree. This has accordingly one real root. But since the degree is even it must have a second real root.

This to all intents rigorous argument is a test of taste. Incidentally the joke is *in* the mathematics, not merely about it.

(10) *Dissection of squares and cubes into squares and cubes, finite in number and all unequal.* The square dissection is possible in an infinity of distinct ways (the simplest is very complicated) , a cube dissection is impossible. The surprising proof of the first result is highly technical. (See

R. L. Brooks, C. A. B. Smith, A. H. Stone and W. T. Tutte, 'The Dissection of Rectangles into Squares,' *Duke Mathematical Journal*, 7 (1940), 312.) The authors give the following elegant proof of the second. In a square dissection the smallest square is not at an edge (for obvious reasons). Suppose now a cube dissection does exist. The cubes standing on the bottom face induce a square dissection of that face, and the smallest of the cubes at the face stands on an internal square. The top face of this cube is enclosed by walls; cubes must stand on this top face; take the smallest—the process continues indefinitely. (It is actually the case that a cube cannot be completely surrounded by larger unequal ones.)

(11) *A voting paradox.* If a man abstains from voting in a General Election on the ground that the chance of his vote's mattering is negligible, it is common to rebuke him by saying 'suppose everyone acted so'. The unpleasant truth that the rebuke is fallacious in principle is perhaps fortunately hidden from the majority of the human race. Consider, however, the magnitudes involved, where the election and the constituency are reasonably open. The chance that his vote will elect his member by a majority of 1 is of the order of 1 in 5000; there is a further chance of the order of 1 in 50 that this result will cause a change of Government. The total chance for this is no worse than 1 in 250,000. Since there are 30,000,000 voters with similar opportunities it would appear that there is something wrong; the explanation is that when the event happens to one man, 20,000 or so [1] other voters in his constituency are in the same position.

A suggestion made in 1909, that two parties in the proportion p to q will have representations as p^3 to q^3, was revived by the *Economist* in January 1950; various earlier elections fit the rule very well. That the proportion is

---

[1] Half 70 per cent. of 60,000.

likely to be magnified is obvious from the fact that if the parties were peppered at random over the country a minority of 49 to 51 would not obtain a single seat. So it is a question of a pattern of localized interests, not of a single mysterious cause.

I am prepared to debunk the rule. In the first place it may be replaced by the simpler one that the percentages $50\pm x$ of the parties should have their difference magnified by a constant c to give representations $50\pm cx$. With $c=3$ the two rules agree substantially up to $x=6$ and then begin to diverge. (With 600 seats a majority 56 : 44 gets 405 seats under the cube rule, 408 under the 3-rule; with 57 : 43 the figures become 420 and 426.) This probably covers all practical cases. (For wider differences one would expect extinction of the minority at some point; the 3-rule predicts it at 67 : 33.) Next, it is not unreasonable that with a given pattern of constituencies there should be a magnification from $50\pm x$ to $50\pm cx$ in the limit as x tends to 0, and this might be extended to work over a range like 0 to 6 of x by the familiar process of cooking c to fit the far end of the range. A change in the constituency-pattern might alter c (the above was written before the election of February 1950, which had a new pattern and a new c). The roundness of the number 3 probably impresses; but unduly, it might almost as easily be 2·9; and after all the velocity of light and the gravitation constant start off with 300 and 666.

(12) *The problems on weighing pennies.* This attractive and 'genuinely mathematical' subject was exhaustively discussed a few years ago, and I will do no more than mention it. (See in particular the masterly analysis by C. A. B. Smith, *Mathematical Gazette*, XXXI (1947), 31-39.)

§ 4. As I explained in § 2 there are things, more 'mathematical' than most of the foregoing, with high claims but omitted on the ground of 'familiarity'. From topology we may mention (13) the Möbius strip, (14) the Klein bottle, (15) the four colour problem, and (16) the Jordan curve problem (the last two are extreme, very extreme, instances where the result is easy to understand while the proof is very difficult). The 'fixed point theorems' belong here (and are discussed in § 5). There is an attractive chapter on topology in *What is Mathematics?* by Courant and Robbins (*CR* for reference), to which the interested reader may be referred.

I mention also, and again without discussion, two pioneering discoveries of Cantor, (17) the non-denumerability of the continuum, and (18) the fact that the points of a line and those of a square are 'similar classes', i.e. can be 'paired off'—put into 'one-one correspondence' (*CR*, 81-85).

(19) The (Schröder-Bernstein) theorem : if a class A is similar to a sub-class A_1 of itself, then it is similar to any ('intermediate') sub-class containing A_1. In this case not only does the result use no more raw material than classes, but there is a proof which brings in no further ideas (except common sense ones like 'all') ; it does not mention numbers, or sequences, and is unaware of the concept 'finite' (and its negation 'infinite'). None the less the proof imposes on this simplest of raw material a technique which is too much for the amateur.

At this point there belong the 'reflexive paradoxes'. For Russell's original contradiction about classes, see *CR*, 87, and for two more see p. 40 below (where they figure under the heading of 'jokes' !).

We now begin to part company more frequently from the amateur, and I will stop numbering.

★ § 5. *An isoperimetrical problem :* an area of (greatest) diameter not greater than 1 is at most $\frac{1}{4}\pi$.

Proofs of various lengths exist. It is easy to see that we may suppose the area convex, and on one side of one of its 'tangents'. With polar co-ordinates as in the figure below

$$\text{area} = \tfrac{1}{2}\int_0^{\frac{1}{2}\pi}(r^2(\theta)+r^2(\theta-\tfrac{1}{2}\pi))d\theta.$$

The integrand is $OP^2+OQ^2=PQ^2\leqslant 1$.

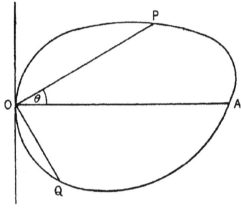

FIG. 2

Suppose $a_n>0$ for all n. Then

$$\varlimsup_{n\to\infty}\left(\frac{1+a_{n+1}}{a_n}\right)^n\geqslant e,$$

and the result is best possible. (From U.S.A.)*

A rod is hinged to the floor of a railway carriage and let go at random ; there is then a small but non-zero probability that, uninterfered with, it will still be standing up at the end of a fortnight : the chance is about 1 in 10^{10^6}. (The train is not an 'ideal' one : it starts e.g. from King's Cross at 3.15, proceeds to a tunnel, where it stops for 5 minutes ; after a dozen or so further stops it reaches Cambridge at 5.35. I seem to remember being told that the genius who asked the original question was unable to answer it.)

There is a proof in *CR*, 319. * Alternatively we may argue (with reasonable latitude of interpretation) as follows. Consider an initial position with the rod (for simplicity) at relative rest and making an angle θ measured from the *left* horizontal (to avoid later clashes of meanings of left and right). Let S be the set of initial positions θ for which the rod sooner or later lies down on the left. Subject to very slight assumptions about the circumstances of the journey and the interaction of train and rod we have the governing fact that *the set S is open* (and we need not try to lay down detailed assumptions). Let θ_0 be the least upper bound of the angles θ of S. Then θ_0 is not a member of S and from initial θ_0 the rod does not lie down on the left. If on the other hand it lies down on the right it will do so also for all θ near enough to θ_0 on the left ; this is false since some (actually all) of these θ belong to S. So from θ_0 the rod never lies down. And for some small enough sector about this θ_0 it will not lie down within a fortnight.

It is instructive to consider why the argument does not similarly prove that the rod, properly started, never moves more than say half a degree from the initial position.*

This argument is instantly convincing to the mathematician. Of possible variants the one chosen seems best suited to be interpreted to the amateur.

Suppose we have any collection S (in general infinite in number) of numbers, or points of a line, ' bounded on the right ' ; that is to say there are points P (far enough to the right) such that no member of S is to the right of P (the statement deliberately contemplates the possibility of a member *coinciding* with P). Any such P is called an upper bound (u.b. for short) of the set S. If the event happens for P it happens (a fortiori) if P is moved to the right. If this event happens for P_0, *but not if P_0 is moved, however little this movement, to the left*, P_0 is called the *least* upper bound (l.u.b.) of S. (E.g. 1 is the l.u.b. of the set of numbers, or again of the set of rational numbers, between 0 and 1, with 1 excluded ; and, again, 1 is the l.u.b. of these two sets modified by 1 being *included*. In the first pair of cases the l.u.b. is not a member of S, in the second pair it is.) After a little mental experiment it should be intuitive that *every set S bounded on the right has a l.u.b.* Note that there are two defining properties of a l.u.b. : (1) it is a u.b., (2) anything to the left is not.

So far the rod-problem has not entered (and the successful reader has acquired an important mathematical conception and theorem). In the argument that follows the various steps can be usefully checked against the special case of the train at rest ; there we know the answer, the rod, started vertical, never moves.

Suppose the rod is started at relative rest at an angle θ measured from the *left* horizontal; call this 'initial position θ'. Consider the set, call it S, of initial positions θ from which the rod lies down sooner or later on the left. If it does this for a particular θ, then *it will do so also for all near enough to it on either side* ; any θ belonging to S is in the middle of a block of θ all belonging to S (in mathematical language 'S is open '). This intuitive fact, on which everything turns, depends on very slight assumptions about the various circumstances, and we need not try to state them in detail.

Let θ_0 be the l.u.b. of the set S. Then θ_0 is not a member of S, for if it were, near enough θ on the right would belong to S and θ_0 would not be an u.b. of S. So the rod, started at θ_0, does not lie down to the left. If on the other hand it lies down to the right, it would do so also from *all* near enough θ on the *left* (the ' open ' principle), so that none of these can be members of S ; this, however, means that θ_0 could be moved to the left without ceasing to be an u.b. of S, contrary to property (2) of a l.u.b. So from θ_0 the rod never lies down. And from some small enough sector round θ_0 it does not lie down within a fortnight.

A similar result is true if the hinge of the rod is replaced by a universal joint. This time, however, we have to appeal to a high-brow 'fixed point theorem' (*CR*, 321).

A typical fixed point theorem is the following. A thin rubber sheet covering the surface of a sphere is deformed without tearing or overlapping. Suppose now further that no point P has its new position P' diametrically opposite its old one. The theorem now is that there must be at least one 'fixed point' (i.e. a P for which P', the 'transform' of P, is the same as P).

The amateur will probably agree that this is elegant (the mathematician says 'beautiful'). But, what he can hardly be expected to realize, it is not only important in itself, but has profound consequences in unexpected fields (like Celestial Mechanics). Importance *plus* simplicity (i.e. simplicity of *result*) give the fixed point theorems very high claims indeed. The status of the *proofs*, however, is something we have not as yet come across. In the first place they took a great deal of finding ; indeed Poincaré, while originating the 'fixed point' conception, stating some of the theorems, and fully aware of their prospective consequences, did not himself *prove* anything. On the other hand the proofs, *once found*, are not beyond the amateur. (There is one in *CR*, see pp. 251-255.)

Is the theorem for the sphere intuitive ?   I think it can be made so. Suppose there is no fixed point (most of the proofs start like this). Then there is a (unique) piece of great circle PP' from each P of the sphere to its transform P', and the direction (from P) varies continuously with P. (Note incidentally that we are here *using* the assumption that P' is not diametrically opposite P ; if it were, the arc PP' would not be unique.) Suppose now that the sphere is covered with hair. If the hair with its root at P is made to fall along PP' the sphere has succeeded in brushing its hair smoothly, with no 'singular' points of 'parting' or 'meeting' : we know intuitively that this is impossible.

So there must be at least 1 singular point, itself not provided with a hair. Contrary to a hasty impression there need not be *more* than 1, this serving as both parting and meeting. Fig. 3 shows how the hair directions run. A dog, which is roughly a topological sphere, makes no attempt to economize in this way; it has a line of parting down its back and one of 'meeting' below.

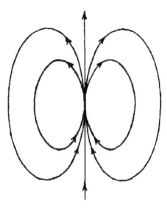

Fig. 3

Every convex closed analytic surface must possess at least two umbilics [1] ($R_1 = R_2 = \infty$ is permitted, and it is possible for there to be only two, and of this kind). The remarkable feature of this theorem is that the only existing proof occupies 180 pages (Hamburger).

§ 6. What is the best stroke ever made in a game of Billiards ? Non-mathematical as this sounds, I claim that, granted the question can be asked significantly, the nature of the answer is deducible by reasoning.[2] It might indeed

---

[1] An umbilic is a point near which the surface is approximately spherical (or plane), the two 'radii of curvature' are equal.

[2] I should be glad to think that when a reader approves of an item he is agreeing with me in finding the 'point' one specially congenial to a mathematician.

be doubted whether the stroke is *possible*, but it did happen that Lindrum, having in the middle of a long break left the object white over a pocket, deliberately played to make a cannon in which the white balls were left touching, and succeeded. (The balls were spotted in accordance with the laws, and the break could continue.)

A flexible inextensible roll (e.g. of film) has its free edge attached horizontally to an inclined plane and uncoils under gravity (Fig. 4). The line of contact has always zero

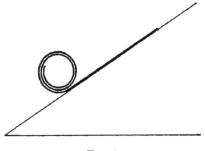

Fig. 4

velocity, and no kinetic energy is destroyed during the motion : when the roll has completely uncoiled there has been a loss of potential energy and the kinetic energy is zero ; what has happened to the missing energy ?

There is an analogy in daily life ; the crack of a whip. With an 'ideal' whip the motion of the tip ends with a finite tension acting on zero mass and the velocity becomes infinite. In practice the velocity does exceed the velocity of sound and a crack results. Perhaps the nearest approach to infinity in everyday life.

A weight is attached to a point of a rough weightless hoop, which then rolls in a vertical plane, starting near the position of unstable equilibrium. What happens, and is it intuitive ?

The hoop lifts off the ground when the radius vector to the weight becomes horizontal. I don't find the lift directly intuitive ; one can, however, ' see ' that the motion is equivalent to the weight's sliding smoothly under gravity on the cycloid it describes, and it is intuitive that it will sooner or later leave *that*. (But the 'seeing' involves the observation that W is instantaneously rotating about P (Fig. 5).)

Mr. H. A. Webb sets the question annually to his engineering pupils, but I don't find it in books.

In actual practice the hoop skids first.

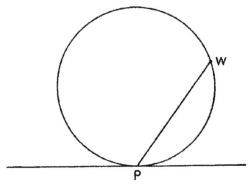

Fig 5

Suppose buses on a given route average 10-minute intervals. If they run at exactly 10-minute intervals the average time a passenger arriving randomly at a stop will have to wait is 5 minutes. If the buses are irregular the average time is greater ; if they are completely random (Gaussian distribution) it is 10 minutes, and, what is more, the average time since the previous bus is also 10 minutes. I understand that London Transport use the deviation from 5 minutes as a criterion of irregular running.

The two things I mention next are alike in that a first guess at the odds is almost certain to be wrong (and they

B

offer opportunities to the unscrupulous). The first has a number of forms (one of them—letters in wrong envelopes— is the source of the sub-factorial notation); the latest is as follows. From two shuffled packs the two top cards are turned up, then the next two, and so on. One bets that sooner or later the pair of cards will be the 'same' (e.g. both 7's of spades). This is fairly well known, but most people who do not know it will offer good odds against; actually the odds are approximately 17 : 10 on (practically $e-1 : 1$).

In the other we have a group of 23 people; what are the odds that some pair of them have the same birthday ? [1] Most people will say the event is unlikely, actually the odds are about evens.

Kakeya's problem. Find the region of least area in which a segment of unit length can turn continuously through 360° (minimize the area swept over). It was long taken for granted that the answer was as in Fig. 6 and the area $\frac{1}{8}\pi$.

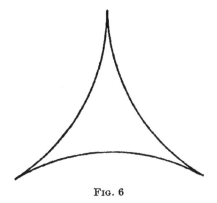

FIG. 6

In 1930, however, A. S. Besicovitch (*Math. Zeit.* 27 (1928), 312-320) showed that the answer is zero area (unattained): given an arbitrarily small ϵ the area swept can be less than ϵ. As ϵ tends to 0 the movements of the segment become

---

[1] In the usual sense : they may have different ages

infinitely complicated and involve excursions towards infinity in all directions.

Crum's problem. What is the maximum number of convex polyhedra of which every pair have a face (or part of one) in common ? In the corresponding problem in 2 dimensions the answer is fairly easily seen to be 4 ; the natural expectation in 3 dimensions is 10 to 12. The answer was given in 1905 by Tietze and rediscovered by Besicovitch in 1947 (*J.L.M.S.* 22, 285-287). In Besicovitch's case it is a foil to his previous problem ; there he annihilated something, here he does the opposite—the answer is infinity.

The question recently arose in conversation whether a dissertation of 2 lines could deserve and get a Fellowship. I had answered this for myself long before ; in mathematics the answer is yes.
* Cayley's projective definition of length is a clear case if we may interpret ' 2 lines ' with reasonable latitude. With Picard's Theorem it could be literally 2, one of statement, one of proof.

[Theorem.]
An integral function never 0 or 1 is a constant.
[Proof.]
    $\exp\{i\Omega(f(z))\}$ is a bounded integral function.
    $[\tau=\Omega(w)$ being inverse to $w=k^2(\tau)]$.

The last bracket is needed solely because of the trivial accident that the function Ω, unlike its inverse $k^2(\tau)$, happens to have no unmistakeable name.*
With Cayley the importance of the idea is obvious at first sight. With Picard the situation is clear enough today (innumerable papers have resulted from it). But I can imagine a referee's report : ' Exceedingly striking and a most original idea. But, brilliant as it undoubtedly is, it

seems more odd than important ; an isolated result, un-related to anything else, and not likely to lead anywhere.'

* Euclid's proof that there is an infinity of primes can be condensed, for the professional, into one line.

'If $p_1, p_2, \cdots, p_n$ are primes, $1 + p_1 p_2 \cdots p_n$ is not divisible by any p_m'.

So can the proof of H. Bohr's famous result that ' $\zeta(s)$ is unbounded in $\sigma > 1$ for large t '.

$$\varlimsup_{\sigma>1,\, t\to\infty} \mathscr{R}\zeta(\sigma+it) \geqslant \varlimsup_{\sigma\to 1+0}\; \varlimsup_{t\to\infty} \Sigma n^{-\sigma} \cos\,(n \log t) = \varlimsup_{\sigma} \Sigma n^{-\sigma} = \infty \text{'}.$$

My last example is a high-brow theorem in analysis. But any mathematician willing to take the importance of the result for granted should be able by judicious skipping to follow the essentials of the proof [2] : this turns on an idea (see the passages in italics) the most impudent in mathe-matics, and brilliantly successful.

A very important theorem (due to M. Riesz) is as follows.

For $a, \beta > 0$ let $M_{a\beta}$ be the least upper bound (u.b. for short) of

$$| L(x, y) | = \left| \sum_{\mu=1}^{m} \sum_{\nu=1}^{n} a_{\mu\nu} x_\mu y_\nu \right|$$

for constant complex $a_{\mu\nu}$ and varying complex x_μ, y_ν subject to

$$\Sigma |x_\mu|^{1/a} \leqslant 1, \quad \Sigma |y_\nu|^{1/\beta} \leqslant 1.$$

Then $\log M_{a\beta}$ is a convex function of a, β (in $a, \beta > 0$).

A convex function of one variable has a graph in which (in the wide sense) ' the arc is below the chord '. With several variables $a, \beta, \ldots$ the function is to be convex in σ on any line l, $a = a_0 + \lambda_1\sigma$, $\beta = \beta_0 + \lambda_2\sigma$, $\ldots$. For the purpose of applications the theorem is extended to a form, T for short, which has a different outward appearance and takes

---

[1] The penultimate step forces the reader to see that ' Dirichlet's theorem ' is being used, and to make the necessary extension of it.

[2] This begins at p. 21, l. 20, and he can take the lemma for granted.

a lot of proving, but the above is the essential foundation. In T the ranges of a and β are extended to include 0, and it then enables us to 'interpolate' in a very drastic manner between a pair of known theorems. Thus, the 'Young-Hausdorff' inequality

$$\left(\Sigma|c_n|^{p/(p-1)}\right)^{(p-1)/p} \leqslant \left(\frac{1}{2\pi}\int_{-\pi}^{\pi}|f|^p d\theta\right)^{1/p}$$

for the Fourier constants c_n of a function $f(\theta)$ of L^p is in fact valid for $1 \leqslant p \leqslant 2$ (with a crude 'interpretation' for $p=1^1$). T enables us to assert the general inequality if only we know it for $p=1$ and $p=2$.[2] For $p=2$ it reduces to Bessel's inequality, and at $p=1$ (such is the power of T) we need to know only the crude form, and this is trivial. T thus produces a high-brow result out of 'nothing'; we experience something like the intoxication of the early days of the method of projecting conics into circles.

Until lately there was no proof of the $M_{a\beta}$ theorem that was not very decidedly difficult. The one I now present is due to G. Thorin ('Convexity Theorems': *Communications du séminaire mathématique de l'Université de Lund*, 9).

We use three immediately obvious principles; (a) the u.b. of a family (possibly infinite in number) of convex functions is convex, (b) a limit of a sequence of convex functions is convex; (c) in finding the u.b. of something subject to a number of independent conditions on the variables we may take the conditions in any order (or simultaneously). E.g. quite generally

$$\underset{0\leqslant x,\, y\leqslant 1}{\text{u.b.}}\ |f(x,\, y)| = \underset{0<x<1}{\text{u.b.}}\ \left(\underset{0<y<1}{\text{u.b.}}\ |f(x,\, y)|\right).$$

It follows from (a) and (c) in combination that if we can express $\log M_{a\beta}$ as

$$\text{u.b.(u.b.(}\ldots\text{(u b.}|L(x,\, y)|)\ldots)),$$

---

[1] Namely 'u.b. $|c_n| \leqslant \frac{1}{2\pi}\int |f|\, d\theta$'.

[2] The l concerned joins the points $(\frac{1}{2},\, \frac{1}{2})$, $(1,\, 0)$, a is $1/p$, β is $(p-1)/p$.

in such a way that the *innermost* u.b. (with all the variables for the outer ones fixed) is convex in (a, β), we shall have proved the theorem. Thorin, however, *takes his (innermost) u.b. with respect to a variable that is not there* !

We must begin with :

Lemma. Suppose that $b_1, b_2, \ldots, b_N$ are real and that $f(s)$ is a finite sum $\Sigma a_r e^{b_r s}$ (or more generally an integral function of $e^{b_1 s}, \ldots, e^{b_N s}$), where $s = \sigma + it$. Let $m(\sigma) = \text{u.b.} |f(s)|$. Then $\log m(\sigma)$ is convex in σ.

By principle (*b*) it is enough to prove this when the *b*'s are rationals β'/β. Then if D is the L.C.M. of the β's, f is an integral function of $z = e^{s/D}$. Hadamard's 'three circles theorem', that '$\log M(r)$ is convex in $\log r$', now gives what we want.

Come now to the theorem. We have to prove $\log M_{\alpha\beta}$ convex on every interval l, or $a = a_0 + \lambda_1 \sigma$, $\beta = \beta_0 + \lambda_2 \sigma$, contained in $a, \beta > 0$. For such a, β we may write

$$x_\mu = \xi_\mu^a e^{i\phi_\mu}, \quad y_\nu = \eta_\nu^\beta e^{i\psi_\nu}, \quad \xi, \eta \geqslant 0 \ ;$$

and then, for varying (real) ϕ, ψ, and (real) ξ, η varying subject to

$$(1)^1 \qquad\qquad \Sigma \xi \leqslant 1, \ \Sigma \eta \leqslant 1, \ \xi, \eta \geqslant 0,$$

we have

$$M_{\alpha\beta} = \underset{(\phi, \psi, \xi, \eta)}{\text{u.b.}} \left(\left| \Sigma\Sigma a_{\mu\nu} \xi_\mu^{a_0 + \lambda_1 \sigma} \eta_\nu^{\beta_0 + \lambda_2 \sigma} e^{i(\phi_\mu + \psi_\nu)} \right| \right).$$

If in this we replace σ by $s = \sigma + it$ (for any real t) the u.b. is unaltered (the maximal $(\phi + \psi)$'s being merely 'translated'). We can now add an operation 'u.b. with respect to t'. By principle (c) we make this the innermost one : summing up and taking logarithms we have

$$\log M_{\alpha\beta} = \underset{(\phi, \psi, \xi, \eta)}{\text{u.b.}} \ \log m(\sigma; \phi, \psi, \xi, \eta),$$

where $$m(\sigma) = \underset{(t)}{\text{u.b.}} \ |f(s)|,$$

$$f(s) = f(s; \phi, \psi, \xi, \eta) = \Sigma\Sigma a \xi^{a_0 + \lambda_1 s} \eta^{\beta_0 + \lambda_2 s} e^{i(\phi + \psi)}.$$

<hr />

[1] These conditions are independent of a, β.

For the range l of a, β (in which the indices are positive), and fixed ϕ, ψ, ξ, η, we can suppress in the sum f any terms in which a ξ or an η is 0 ; *the modified f has the form of the f in the lemma, $\log m(\sigma)$ is convex for all σ, and in particular for the range concerned.* $\log M_{a\beta}$ *is now convex in σ by principle* (a).★

§ 7. *Ciphers.* The legend that every cipher [1] is breakable is of course absurd, though still widespread among people who should know better. I give a sufficient example, without troubling about its precise degree of practicability. Suppose we have a 5-figure number N. Starting at a place N in a 7-figure log-table take a succession of pairs of digits $d_1 d'_1$, $d_2 d'_2$, . from the last figures of the entries. Take the remainder of the 2-figure number $d_n d_n'$ after division by 26. This gives a 'shift' s_n, and the code is to shift [2] the successive letters of the message by s_1, s_2,.. respectively.

It is sufficiently obvious that a *single* message cannot be unscrambled, and this even if all were known except the key number N (indeed the triply random character of s_n is needlessly elaborate). If the same code is used for a number of messages it could be broken, but all we need do is to vary N. It can be made to depend on a date, given in clear ; the key might e.g. be that N is the first 5 figures of the 'tangent' of the date (read as degrees, minutes, seconds : 28° 12′ 52″ for Dec. 28, 1952). This rule could be carried in the head, with nothing on paper to be stolen or betrayed. If any one thinks there is a possibility of the entire scheme being guessed he could modify 26 to 21 and use a date one week earlier than the one given in clear.

---

[1] I am using the word cipher as the plain man understands it.
[2] A shift of $s=2$ turns ' k ' into ' m ', ' z ' into ' b '.

From the Mathematical Tripos

§ 8.   It is always pleasant to find others doing the silly things one does oneself.   The following appears as a complete question in Schedule B for 1924 (Paper I).

(a) [1] An ellipsoid surrounded by frictionless homogeneous liquid begins to move in any direction with velocity V. Show that if the outer boundary of the liquid is a fixed confocal ellipsoid, the momentum set up in the liquid is $-MV$, where M is the mass of the liquid displaced by the ellipsoid.

[The result was later extended to other pairs of surfaces, e.g. two coaxial surfaces of revolution.]

Whatever the two surfaces are we can imagine the inner one to be filled with the same liquid ; then the centre of mass does not move.

Published sets of examination questions contain (for good reasons) not what was set but what ought to have been set ; a year with no correction is rare.   One year a question was so impossibly wrong that we substituted a harmless dummy.

There used to be ' starred ' questions in Part II (present style), easy, and not counting towards a 1st.   A proposed starred question was once rejected, proposed and rejected as too hard for an unstarred one, and finally used as a question in Part III.

Once when invigilating I noticed, first that the logarithm tables provided did not give values either for e or for $\log e = \cdot 4343$, secondly that question 1 asked for a proof that

---

[1] Let the amateur read bravely on.

something had the numerical value 4·343 (being in fact $10 \log e$). Was I to announce the missing information, thereby giving a lead ?   After hesitation I did so, and by oversight committed the injustice of not transmitting the information to the women candidates, who sat elsewhere.

§ 9.   I inherited Rouse Ball's ' Examiner's books ' for the Triposes of round about 1881. In passing, some details may be of interest. The examination was taken in January of the 4th year. In one year full marks were 33,541, the Senior Wrangler got 16,368, the second 13,188, the last Wrangler 3123, the Wooden Spoon (number ninety odd) 247.   The first question carried $6+15$ marks, the last question of the 2nd-4-days problem paper 325 (>247).

As a staunch opponent of the old Tripos I was slightly disconcerted to find a strong vein of respectability running throughout. It is surprising to discover that a man who did all the bookwork (which was much the same as it is now) and nothing else would have been about 23rd Wrangler out of 30.   Since even the examiners of the '80's sometimes yielded to the temptation to set a straightforward application of the bookwork as a rider, he would pick up some extra marks, which we may suppose would balance occasional lapses. The two heavily marked problem papers contained of course no bookwork for him to do ; if we suppose that he scored a quarter of the marks of the Senior for these papers, or say 7 per cent. of the total, he would go up to about 20th. (Round about 1905 the figures would be 14th Wrangler out of 26 for pure bookwork, rising to 11th on 7 per cent. of the problem papers, and incidentally straddling J. M. Keynes.)

§ 10.   On looking through the questions, and especially the problem papers, for high virtuosity (preferably vicious) I was again rather disappointed ; two questions, however, have stuck in my memory.

(*b*) A sphere spinning in equilibrium on top of a rough horizontal cylinder is slightly disturbed ; prove that the track of the point of contact is initially a helix.

* Pursuing this idea an examiner in the following year produced (Jan. 18, morning, 1881, my wording).

(*c*) If the sphere has a centrally symmetrical law of density such as to make the radius of gyration a certain fraction of the radius then, whatever the spin, the track is a helix so long as contact lasts. [Marked at 200 ; a second part about further details carried another 105.]*

The question about (*b*) is whether it can, like (*a*), be debunked.   On a walk shortly after coming across (*b*) and (*c*) I sat down on a tree trunk near Madingley for a rest. Some process of association called up question (*b*), and the following train of thought flashed through my mind. ' Initially a helix ' means that the curvature and the torsion are stationary at the highest point P ; continue the track backwards ; there is skew-symmetry about P, hence the curvature and torsion are stationary.   I now ask : is this a proof, or the basis of one, how many marks should I get, and how long do you take to decide the point ?

* § 11.   Proceed to (*c*).   I do not regard this question [1] as vicious : it involves the general principles of moving axes with geometrical conditions , a queer coincidence makes the final equations soluble, but this is easy to spot with the result given.   The extremely elegant result seems little known.

Take moving axes at the centre of the sphere with Oy along the normal to the point of contact, making an angle, θ say, with the vertical, and Oz parallel to the cylinder.

---

[1] The actual question gave the law of density and left the radius of gyration to be calculated, and asked for some further details of the motion.

Eliminating the reactions at the point of contact we get (cp. Lamb, *Higher Mechanics*, 165-166) :

$$(I+Ma^2)b\theta=Ma^2g \sin \theta,$$
$$(I+Ma^2)\dot{w}=Ia \; \theta q,$$
$$aq+w\dot{\theta}=0,$$

which, on normalizing to $a=1$, become respectively, say,

$$\lambda\ddot{\theta}=\sin \theta, \; \mu^2 w=\dot{\theta}q, \; q=-w\theta.$$

The 2nd and 3rd of these lead to,

$$q=n \cos (\theta/\mu), \; \mu w=n \sin (\theta/\mu),$$

where n is the initial spin. If $\mu=2$ these combine with the first to give $w=\frac{1}{4}n\lambda\theta$ and so $z=\frac{1}{4}n\lambda\theta$.*

Suppose a sphere is started rolling on the inside of a rough *vertical* cylinder (gravity acting, but no dissipative forces) ; what happens ? The only sensible guess is a spiral descent of increasing steepness ; actually the sphere moves up and down between two fixed horizontal planes. Golfers are not so unlucky as they think.

Some time about 1911 an examiner A proposed the question. E and W are partners at Bridge ; suppose E, with no ace, is given the information that W holds an ace, what is the probability p that he holds 2 at least ? A colleague B, checking A's result, got a different answer, q. On analysis it appeared that B calculated the probability, q, that W has 2 aces at least given that he has the spade ace. p and q are not the same, and $q>p$.

Subject always to E's holding no ace, $1-q$ is the probability of W holding S ace only, divided by the probability of his holding at least S ace ; $1-p$ is the probability of his holding 1 ace only, divided by the probability of his holding at least 1 ace. The 2nd numerator is 4 times the 1st. Hence

$$\frac{1-p}{1-q} = \frac{\text{(probability of S ace at least)} + \cdots + \text{(probability of C ace at least)}}{\text{(probability of 1 ace at least)}}$$

Since the contingencies in the numerator overlap, this ratio is greater than 1.

The fallacy '$p=q$' arises by the argument : 'W has an ace ; we may suppose it is the spade '. But there is no such thing as ' it ' ; if W has more than one the informer has to *choose* one to be ' it '. The situation becomes clearer when a hand of 2 cards is dealt from the 3 cards, S ace, H ace, C 2. Here we know in any case that the hand has an ace, and the probability of 2 aces is $\frac{1}{3}$. If we know the hand has the S ace the probability of 2 aces is $\frac{1}{2}$.

Cross-purposes, unconscious assumptions, howlers, misprints, etc.

§ 12. A good, though non-mathematical, example is the child writing with its left hand ' because God the Father does '. (He has to; the Son is sitting on the other one.)

I once objected to an apparently obscure use of the phrase ' let us suppose for simplicity '. It should mean that the writer could do the unsimplified thing, but wishes to let the reader off; it turned out that my pupil meant that he had to simplify before *he* could do it

It is of course almost impossible to guard against unconscious assumptions. I remember reading the description of the coordinate axes in Lamb's *Higher Mechanics*: Ox and Oy as in 2 dimensions, Oz vertical. For me this is quite wrong; Oz is horizontal (I work always in an armchair with my feet up).

How would the reader present the picture of a closed curve (e.g. a circle) lying entirely to one side of one of it's tangents? There are 4 schools; I belong to that of a vertical tangent with the curve on the right; I once referred to the configuration, and without a figure, in terms that made nonsense for the other 3 schools.

How not to

A brilliant but slapdash mathematician once enunciated a theorem in 2 parts, adding : ' part 2, which is trivial, is due to Hardy and Littlewood '.

The trivial part 2 needed to be stated ' for completeness ', and Hardy and Littlewood had similarly needed to state it. The author had then to comply with the rule that nothing

29

previously published may be stated without due acknowledgement.

In presenting a mathematical argument the great thing is to give the educated reader the chance to catch on at once to the momentary point and take details for granted : his successive mouthfuls should be such as can be swallowed at sight ; in case of accidents, or in case he wishes for once to check in detail, he should have only a clearly circumscribed little problem to solve (e.g. to check an identity . *two* trivialities omitted can add up to an *impasse*). The unpractised writer, even after the dawn of a conscience, gives him no such chance , before he can spot the point he has to tease his way through a maze of symbols of which not the tiniest suffix can be skipped   I give below an example (from analysis, where the most serious trouble occurs).   This is not at all extreme for a draft before it has been revised by some unfortunate supervisor or editor.   It is unduly favourable to the criminal since the main point is hard to smother.   But it is not easy to be interestingly boring, and in momentary default of a specimen of the genuine article it is the best I can do.   (There is a game of selecting a team of the 11 most conspicuous representatives of a given quality : who are the 11 most brilliantly dim persons ?   My choice is too blasphemous, seditious and libellous to quote)

* A famous theorem of Weierstrass says that a function $f(x_1, x_2)$ continuous in a rectangle R, can be uniformly approximated to by a sequence of polynomials in x_1, x_2. It is valid in n dimensions, and the beginner will give what follows, but in $x_1, x_2, \ldots, x_n$; $x_1', x_2', \ldots, x_n'$. The proof, an audacious combination of ideas, is in 2 parts ;   the second cannot be badly mauled and I give it at the end. Here is the beginner's proof of the first part.   I am indebted to Dr. Flett for one or two happy misimprovements, and for additional realism have left some incidental misprints uncorrected.

With $f(x_1, x_2)$ continuous in $(-a \leqslant x_1 \leqslant a, -b \leqslant x_2 \leqslant b)$, let $c > 0$ and define a function $f_1(x_1, x_2)$ by

$$
f_1(x_1, x_2) = \begin{cases}
f(-a, b) \ (-c-a \leqslant x_1 \leqslant -a, b \leqslant x_2 \leqslant b+c) \\
f(x_1, b) \ (-a \leqslant x_1 \leqslant a, b \leqslant x_2 \leqslant b+c) \\
f(a, b) \ (-a \leqslant x_1 \leqslant a+c, b \leqslant x_2 \leqslant b+c) \\
f(-a, x_2) \ (-a-c \leqslant x_1 \leqslant -a, -b \leqslant x_2 \leqslant b) \\
f(x_1, x_2) \ (-a \leqslant x_1 \leqslant a, -b \leqslant x_2 \leqslant b) \\
f(a, x_2) \ (a \leqslant x_1 \leqslant a+c, -b \leqslant x_2 \leqslant b) \\
f(a, -b) \ (-a-c \leqslant x_1 \leqslant -a, -b-c \leqslant x_2 \leqslant -b) \\
f(x_1, -b) \ (-a \leqslant x_1 \leqslant a, -b-c \leqslant x_2 \leqslant -b) \\
f(-a, -b) \ (-a-c \leqslant x_1 \leqslant -a, -b-c \leqslant x_2 \leqslant -b).
\end{cases}
$$

It can easily be shown that $f_1(x_1, x_2)$ is continuous in

$$(-a-c \leqslant x_1 \leqslant a+c, -b-c \leqslant x_2 \leqslant b+c).$$

For points (x_1, x_2) of R define

$$\phi_n(x_1, x_2) = \pi^{-1} n \int_{-a-c}^{a+c} dx'_1 \int_{-b-c}^{b+c} f_1(x'_1, y'_1) \exp[-n\{(x'_1 - x_1)^2 + (y'_1 - y_1)^2\}] dx'_2.$$

We shall show [this is the first half referred to above] that

(1) $\phi_n(x_1, x_2) \to f(x_1, x_2)$ as $n \to \infty$, uniformly for (x_1, x_2) of R.

There is a $\delta(\epsilon)$ such that $|f_1(x_1'', x_2'') - f_1(x_1', x_2')| < \epsilon$ provided that (x_1', x_2') and (x_1'', x_2'') belong to $(-a-c \leqslant x_1' \leqslant a+c, -b-c \leqslant x_2' \leqslant b+c)$ and satisfy $|x_1'' - x_1'| < \delta(\epsilon)$ and $|x_2'' - x_2'| < \delta(\epsilon)$. Let

$$n_0 = n_0(\epsilon) = \text{Max } ([c^3]+1, [\delta^{-3}(\epsilon)]+1),$$

and let $n > n_0$. Then $-a-c < x_1 - n^{-\frac{1}{3}} < x_1 + n^{-\frac{1}{3}} < a+c$, $-b-c < x_2 - n^{-\frac{1}{3}} < x_2 + n^{-\frac{1}{3}} < b+c$, and we have

$$\phi_n(x_1, x_2) = \pi^{-1} n \left[\int_{-a+c}^{a+c} dx_1' \int_{x_1+n^{-\frac{1}{3}}}^{b+c} dx_2' + \int_{-a-c}^{a+c} dx_1' \int_{x_1-n^{-\frac{1}{3}}}^{x_1+n^{-\frac{1}{3}}} dx_2' + \int_{x_1-n^{-\frac{1}{3}}}^{x_1+n^{-\frac{1}{3}}} dx_1' \int_{x_1-n^{-\frac{1}{3}}}^{x_1+n^{-\frac{1}{3}}} dx_2' \right.$$

$$\left. + \int_{x_1+n^{-\frac{1}{3}}}^{a+c} dx_1' \int_{x_1-n^{-\frac{1}{3}}}^{x_1+n^{-\frac{1}{3}}} dx_2' + \int_{-a-c}^{a+c} dx_1' \int_{-b-c}^{x_1-n^{-\frac{1}{3}}} dx_2' \right] f_1(x_1', x_2') \exp[-n\{(x_1'-n_1)^2 + (x_2'-x_2)^2\}]$$

(2) $=T_1+T_2+\cdots+T_5$,

say. In T_1 we have $|f_1(x_1', x_2')|<K$, $\exp[\ ]\leqslant\exp(-n.n^{-\frac{2}{3}})$, and so

(3) $|T_1|<\epsilon(n>n_1(\epsilon))$.

Similarly [1]

(4) $|T_2|$, $|T_4|$, $|T_5|<\epsilon$ $(n>n_2(\epsilon))$.

In T_3 write $x_1'=x_1+x_1''$, $x_2'=x_2+x_2''$.   Since $|x_1''|\leqslant n^{-\frac{1}{3}}$, $|x_2''|\leqslant n^{-\frac{1}{3}}$ in the range concerned we have

(5) $|f_1(x_1+x_1'', x_2+x_2'')-f_1(x_1, x_2)|<\epsilon\ (n>\delta^{-3}(\epsilon))$.

Now in T_3 we have $f_1(x_1, x_2)=f(x_1, x_2)$.   Hence

(6) $T_3=T_{3,1}+T_{3,2}$, where

(7) $T_{3,1}=\pi^{-1}nf(x_1, x_2)\int_{-n^{-\frac{1}{3}}}^{n^{-\frac{1}{3}}}dx_1''\int_{-n^{-\frac{1}{3}}}^{n^{-\frac{1}{3}}}dx_2''\exp\left[-n(x_1''^2+x_2''^2)\right]$,

(8) $T_{3,2}=\pi^{-1}n\int_{-n^{-\frac{1}{3}}}^{n^{-\frac{1}{3}}}dx_1''\int_{-n^{-\frac{1}{3}}}^{n^{-\frac{1}{3}}}dx_2''\epsilon\{f_1(x_1+x_1'', x_2+x_2'')-f_1(x_1, x_2)\}$

$\exp\left[-n(x_1''^2+x_2''^2)\right]$.

We have, for $n>\mathrm{Max}(n_0, n_1, n_2)$,

(9) $|T_{3,2}|\leqslant\pi^{-1}n\int_{-n^{-\frac{1}{3}}}^{n^{-\frac{1}{3}}}dx_1''\int_{-n^{-\frac{1}{3}}}^{n^{-\frac{1}{3}}}dx_2''\epsilon\exp\left[-n(x_1''^2+x_2''^2)\right]$

$\leqslant\pi^{-1}\epsilon n\int_{-\infty}^{\infty}dx_1''\int_{-\infty}^{\infty}dx_2''\exp\left[-n(x_1''^2+x_2''^2)\right]=\epsilon$.

Also the double integral in (7) is

(10) $\left(\int_{-n^{-\frac{1}{3}}}^{n^{-\frac{1}{3}}}e^{-nu^2}du\right)^2$

[1] I disclose at this point that in $T_2\int_{-a-c}^{a+c}$ is a 'slip' for $\int_{-a-c}^{x_1-n^{-\frac{1}{3}}}$. One slip is practically certain in this style of writing, generally devil-inspired.

Now
$$\int_{-n^{-\frac{1}{6}}}^{n^{-\frac{1}{6}}} e^{-nu^2}du = 2\int_0^{n^{-\frac{1}{6}}} = 2\int_0^\infty - 2\int_{n^{-\frac{1}{6}}}^\infty$$

$$= n^{-\frac{1}{2}}\pi^{\frac{1}{2}} - 2\int_0^\infty e^{-n(n^{-\frac{1}{6}}+t)^2}dt$$

$$= n^{-\frac{1}{2}}\pi^{\frac{1}{2}} + O\left(e^{-n^{\frac{1}{6}}}\int_0^\infty e^{-2n^{\frac{3}{6}}t}dt\right)$$

$$= n^{-\frac{1}{2}}\pi^{\frac{1}{2}}\left(1 + O\left(n^{-\frac{1}{6}}e^{-n^{\frac{1}{6}}}\right)\right).$$

Hence it is easily seen that

$$\left|\left(\int_{-n^{-\frac{1}{6}}}^{n^{-\frac{1}{6}}} e^{-nu^2}du\right)^2 - n^{-1}\pi\right| = \left|n^{-1}\pi\{1 + O(n^{-\frac{1}{6}}e^{-n^{\frac{1}{6}}})\} - n^{-1}\pi\right|$$
$$< \epsilon \ (n > n_3(\epsilon)).$$

Hence from (10) and (7)

(11) $|T_{3,1} - f(x_1, x_2)| < K\epsilon \ (n > \text{Max}(n_0, n_1, n_2, n_3))$.
From (2) to (11) it follows that
$\quad |\phi_n(x_1, x_2) - f(x_1, x_2)| < K\epsilon \ (n > \text{Max}(n_0, n_1, n_2, n_3))$,
and we have accordingly proved (1).

A civilized proof is as follows.
Extend the definition of $f(x, y)$ to a larger rectangle R_+; e.g. on AB f is to be $f(A)$, and in the shaded square it is to be $f(C)$. The new f is continuous in R_+. Define, for (x, y) of R,

(i) $\qquad \phi_n(x, y) = \iint_{R_+} f(\xi, \eta)\text{E}d\xi d\eta \bigg/ \int_{-\infty}^\infty \int_{-\infty}^\infty \text{E}d\xi d\eta$,

where $\text{E} = \exp[-n\{(\xi-x)^2 + (\eta-y)^2\}]$. The denominator is the constant πn^{-1} (independent of x, y); hence (i) is equivalent to

(ii) $\qquad \phi_n(x, y) = \pi^{-1}n\iint_{R_+} f(\xi, \eta)\text{E}d\xi d\eta$.

The contributions to the numerator and to the denominator in (i) of (ξ, η)'s outside the square $S = S(x, y)$ of side $n^{-\frac{1}{6}}$

C

round (x, y) are exponentially small. The denominator itself being πn^{-1} we have (o's uniform)

$$\phi_n(x, y) = \left(\iint_S f(\xi, \eta) \mathrm{E} d\xi d\eta \Big/ \iint_S \mathrm{E} d\xi d\eta \right) + o(1).$$

S being small, the $f(\xi, \eta)$ in the last numerator is $f(x, y) + o(1)$; so finally the ϕ_n defined by (ii) satisfies $\phi_n(x, y) = f(x, y) + o(1)$ as desired.

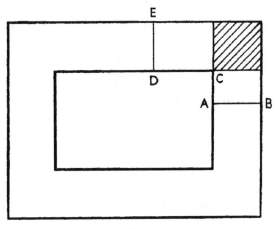

Fig. 7

The second part of the proof of Weierstrass's theorem is as follows. For a suitable $N = N(n)$ we have, for all x, y of R and all ξ, η of R_+,

$$|\mathrm{E} - \Sigma| < n^{-2},$$

where

$$\Sigma = \sum_{m=0}^{N} \frac{[-n\{(\xi-x)^2 + (\eta-y)^2\}]^m}{m!}$$

Then

$$\phi_n(x, y) = \Pi + o(1),$$

where $\Pi = \pi^{-1} n \iint_{R_+} \Sigma d\xi d\eta$, and is evidently a polynomial in (x, y).

Early writers had of course to work with what we should find intolerably clumsy tools and notations. An extreme case is a proof by Cauchy that every equation has a root. The modern version given in Hardy's *Pure Mathematics* (9th Edition, 494-496) could if necessary be telescoped to half a page. The ideas are all in Cauchy, but the reference to him has to be '*Exercises*, t. 4, 65-128': 64 pages (and all relevant, even though Cauchy is doing much pioneering by the way). The reading is not made any lighter by the fact that what we should call $\sum_0^n b_m'' z^m$ has to appear as

$$(D_0'' + E_0'' \sqrt{-1}) + (D_1'' + E_1'' \sqrt{-1})(x + y\sqrt{-1}) + \ldots$$
$$+ (D_n'' + E_n'' \sqrt{-1})(x + y\sqrt{-1})^n.$$

Post-script on pictures

The ' pictorial' definition by Fig. 7, while the natural *source* of the idea, could in point of fact be given verbally with almost equal immediacy : ' define f outside R to have the value at the nearest point of R '; this would be used in a printed paper if only to save expense, but the picture in a lecture. Here it serves as text for a sermon. My pupils *will* not use pictures, even unofficially and when there is no question of expense. This practice is increasing ; I have lately discovered that it has existed for 30 years or more, and also why. A heavy warning used to be given [1] that pictures are not rigorous ; this has never had its bluff called and has permanently frightened its victims into playing for safety. Some pictures are of course not rigorous, but I should say most are (and I use them whenever possible myself). An obviously legitimate case is to use a graph to define an awkward function (e.g. behaving differently in successive stretches) : I recently had to plough through a definition quite comparable with the ' bad ' one above, where a graph would have told the story in a matter of

---

[1] To break with ' school mathematics '.

seconds. *This* sort of pictoriality does not differ in status from a convention like ' SW corner ', now fully acclimatized. But pictorial *arguments*, while not so purely conventional, can be quite legitimate. Take the theorem [1] : ' $f(x)=o(1)$ as $x \rightarrow \infty$ and $f''=O(1)$ imply $f'=o(1)$ '. If $f' \neq o(1)$ the graph $y=f'(x)$ will for some arbitrarily large x have ' peaks ' (above or below $y=0$) enclosing triangles like PQR, the height of P not small, the slopes of PQ, PR not large, and so the area PQR not small. Then $f(Q)-f(R)$ is not small, contradicting $f=o(1)$. This is rigorous (and printable), in the sense that

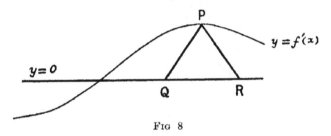

Fɪɢ 8

in translating into symbols no step occurs that is not both unequivocal and trivial. For myself I *think* like this wherever the subject matter permits.

Probably the best of pictorial arguments is a proof of the ' fixed point theorem ' in 1 dimensions : *Let $f(x)$ be continuous and increasing in $0 \leqslant x \leqslant 1$, with values satisfying $0 \leqslant f(x) \leqslant 1$, and let $f_2(x)=f\{f(x)\}$, $f_n(x)=f\{f_{n-1}(x)\}$. Then under iteration of f every point is either a fixed point, or else converges to a fixed point.*

For the professional the only proof needed is Fig. 9.*

(Via Dr. A. E. Western.) There was a Rent Act after 1914, and the definition of when a house was subject to it was as follows (my notation in brackets). The ' standard

---

[1] ' Not, alas, by J. E. Littlewood ', though my rediscovery of it was an important moment in my career. I mention it because I got it by using the picture.

rent ' (R) was defined to be the rent in 1914 (R_0), unless this was less than the rateable value (V), in which case it was to be the rateable value. ' The house is subject to the act if either the standard rent or the rateable value is less

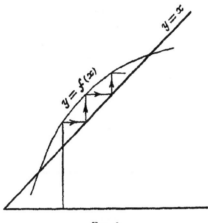

Fig. 9

than £105.' There were many law suits, argued *ad hoc* in each case. The subject is governed by a fundamental theorem, unknown to the Law :

Theorem : The house is subject to the act if and only if $V < 105$.

This follows from [1]

Lemma. $\text{Min}\{\text{Max}(R_0,\ V),\ V\} = V$.

§ 13. *Misprints.* A recent number of the *Observatory* contained the charming ' typicle partical '.

Professor Offord and I recently committed ourselves to an odd mistake (*Annals of Mathematics* (2), 49, 923, 1.5). In formulating a proof a plus sign got omitted, becoming in

[1] Min (a, b) means the smaller, Max (a, b) the larger, of a and b.

effect a multiplication sign. The resulting false formula got accepted as a basis for the ensuing fallacious argument. (In defence, the final result was known to be true.)

In the *Mathematical Gazette* XIV, 23, there is a note on ' Noether's Canonical Curves ', by W. P. Milne, in which he refers to ' a paper by Guyaelf (*Proc. London Math. Soc.*, Ser. 2, 21, part 5) '. Guyaelf is a ghost-author ; the paper referred to is by W. P. Milne.

I once challenged Hardy to find a misprint on a certain page of a joint paper : he failed. It was in his own name : ' G, H. Hardy '.

A minute I wrote (about 1917) for the Ballistic Office ended with the sentence ' Thus σ should be made as small as possible '. This did not appear in the printed minute. But P. J. Grigg said, ' what is that ? ' A speck in a blank space at the end proved to be the tiniest σ I have ever seen (the printers must have scoured London for it).

In Music a misprint can turn out to be a stroke of genius (perhaps the A$\sharp$ in bar 224 of the first movement of Beethoven's opus 106). Could this happen in Mathematics ? I can imagine a hypothetical case. There was a time when infinite sets of intervals were unthought of, and a ' set of intervals ' would be taken to mean a finite set. Suppose a definition of the ' content ' of a set of points E, ' the lower bound of the total length of a set of intervals enclosing E '. Suppose now some precisian, supplying the missing ' finite ', should be moved to ask himself 'suppose an infinite set *were* allowed ? ' He would have set foot on a road leading inevitably to Lebesgue measure.

§ 14. *Verbalities.* I once came on a phrase like ' this will be true of the classes A, B, C provided C is not overlapped by A nor B '. The writer had queried the ' nor ' but was told by a literary friend that it was necessary. It is obviously impossible mathematically : why ? (The ' or ' in ' A or B ' is a mathematical symbol ; ' A or B ' is the mathematical name of a ' sum-class '.)

A recent (published) paper had near the beginning the passage ' the object of this paper is to prove [something very important] '. It transpired [1] with great difficulty, and not till near the end, that the ' object ' was an unachieved one.[2]

From an excellent book on Astronomy. ' Many of the spirals [galaxies], but very few of the ellipsoidals, show bright lines due, no doubt, to the presence or absence of gaseous nebulae.'
[This rich complex of horrors repays analysis. Roughly it is an illegitimate combination of the correct ' spirals show bright lines due to the presence . . . ' and the incorrect ' ellipsoidals don't show bright lines due to the absence . . .'.]

The literary convention that numbers less than 10 should be given in words is often highly unsuitable in mathematics (though delicate distinctions are possible). The excessive use of the word forms is regrettably spreading at the present time. I lately came across (the lowest depth, from a very naive writer) ' functions never taking the values nought or one '. I myself favour using figures practically always (and am acting up to the principle in the book).

A linguist would be shocked to learn that if a set is not closed this does not mean that it is open, or again that ' E is dense in E ' does not mean the same thing as ' E is dense in itself '.

---

[1] I have often thought that a good literary competition would be to compose a piece in which all the normal misuses of words and constructions were at first sight committed, but on consideration not.

[2] The author intended no unfulfilled claim, but his use of language was unusual.

' More than one is ' · ' fewer than two are '.

' Where big X is very small.'

I considered including some paradoxical effects of the word ' nothing ', but on consideration the thing is too easy.

The spoken word has dangers. A famous lecture was unintelligible to most of its audience because ' Hárnoo ', clearly an important character in the drama, failed to be identified in time as $h\nu$.

I have had occasion to read aloud the phrase ' where E' is any dashed (i.e. derived) set ' : it is necessary to place the stress with care.

Jokes, etc.

§ 15. All the reflexive paradoxes are of course admirable jokes. Well-known as they are, I will begin with two classical ones.

(*a*) (Richard). There must exist (positive) integers that cannot be named in English by fewer than nineteen [1] syllables. Every collection of positive integers contains a least member, and there is a number N, ' the least integer not nameable in fewer than nineteen syllables '. But this phrase contains 18 syllables, and defines N.

(*b*) (Weyl). The vast majority of English adjectives do not *possess* the quality they *denote* ; the adjective ' red ' is not red · some, however, do possess it ; e.g. the adjective ' adjectival '. Call the first kind heterological, the second homological : every adjective is one or the other. ' Heterological ' is an adjective ; which is it ?

In a *Spectator* competition the following won a prize ; subject : what would you most like to read on opening the morning paper ?

[1] Not ' 19 ', for sufficient if delicate reasons.

OUR SECOND COMPETITION

The First Prize in the second of this year's competitions goes to Mr. Arthur Robinson, whose witty entry was easily the best of those we received. His choice of what he would like to read when opening his paper was headed, 'Our Second Competition', and was as follows : 'The First Prize in the second of this year's competitions goes to Mr. Arthur Robinson, whose witty entry was easily the best of those we received. His choice of what he would like to read on opening his paper was headed 'Our Second Competition', but owing to paper restrictions we cannot print all of it.'

Reflexiveness flickers delicately in and out of the latter part of Max Beerbohm's story *Enoch Soames*.

The following idea, a coda to the series, was invented too late (I do not remember by whom), but what *should* have happened is as follows. I wrote a paper for the *Comptes Rendus* which Prof. M. Riesz translated into French for me. At the end there were 3 footnotes. The first read (in French) 'I am greatly indebted to Prof. Riesz for translating the present paper'. The second read 'I am indebted to Prof. Riesz for translating the preceding footnote'. The third read 'I am indebted to Prof. Riesz for translating the preceding footnote', with a suggestion of reflexiveness. Actually I stop legitimately at number 3 . however little French I know I am capable of *copying* a French sentence.

Schoolmaster : 'Suppose x is the number of sheep in the problem'. Pupil : 'But, Sir, suppose x is not the number of sheep'. [I asked Prof. Wittgenstein was this not a profound philosophical joke, and he said it was.]

(A. S. Besicovitch) A mathematician's reputation rests on the number of bad proofs he has given. (Pioneer work is clumsy.)

' The surprising thing about this paper is that a man who *could* write it—would.'

' I should like to say how much this paper owes to Mr. Smith.' ' Then why not do so ? '

Equivalence and identity
How many use the symbolism $O(1)$ without realizing that there is a tacit convention ? It is true that $\sin x = O(1)$; but it is not true that $O(1) = \sin x$.

' Honesty is the best policy ' Very well then ; if I act so as to do the best for myself I am assured of acting honestly.

From time to time (since 1910) there were moves to get rid of the revolting optics and astronomy set in the Mathematical Tripos It was discovered that over a period of years no wrangler attempted a question in either subject. An equivalent form of this proposition is that every attempt to do a question in optics or astronomy resulted in a failure to get a 1st.

' We all know that people can sometimes do better things than they have done, but ——— has done a better thing than he can do.' [An actual case, with agreement on the point among experts.]

An over-anxious research student was asking whether it was necessary to read all the literature before trying his hand. ' *Nothing* is necessary—or sufficient.' The second part (embodying a harsh truth ; the infinitely competent can be uncreative) arises inevitably by purely verbal association.

' Don't sniff at the sonatas of Archdukes, you never know who wrote them ' (Haydn). [A propos of a rejected Ph.D. thesis.]

A too-persistent research student drove his supervisor to say ' Go away and work out the construction for a regular

polygon of 65537 $[=2^{16}+1]$ sides '. The student returned
20 years later with a construction (deposited in the Archives
at Góttingen).

A less painful story, which I certainly heard 25 or more
years ago but will not vouch for the truth of, is that the
first use of a crystal as a diffraction lattice was the result of
taking seriously a suggestion made in jest. Such things
could obviously happen. (I remember saying myself, on
the theme that one should not impart prejudices from daily
life into, say, astrophysics: ' be prepared to treat the sun as
rigid or the interior of the earth as a perfect gas '. This was
at a time when the stars were supposed to be at best very
imperfect gases.)

Charles Darwin had a theory that once in a while one
should perform a damn-fool experiment. It almost always
fails, but when it does come off is terrific.

Darwin played the trombone to his tulips. The result of
this particular experiment was negative.

' X finds gravitational waves in these conditions, but
there is a suggestion that there is a mistake in the work.'
' Clearly *any* mistake generates gravitational waves.'

Landau kept a printed form for dealing with proofs of
Fermat's last theorem. ' On page blank, lines blank to
blank, you will find there is a mistake.' (Finding the mistake
fell to the Privat Dozent.)

A precisian professor had the habit of saying : ' . . .
quartic polynomial $ax^4+bx^3+cx^2+dx+e$, where e need not
be the base of the natural logarithms '. (It might be.)

It was said of Jordan's writings that if he had 4 things
on the same footing (as a, b, c, d) they would appear as a,
M_3', ϵ_2, $\Pi_{1,2}''$.

' Liable to create a true impression.' (E.g. faking in an
examination.)

' Less in this than meets the eye.'

Rock-climbing angles (*c.* 1900).
    Perpendicular—60°.
    My dear Sir, absolutely perpendicular—65°.
    Overhanging—70°.

I read in the proof-sheets of Hardy on Ramanujan : ' as someone said, each of the positive integers was one of his personal friends '. My reaction was, " I wonder who said that ; I wish I had ". In the next proof-sheets I read (what now stands), ' it was Littlewood who said . . .'.

[What had happened was that Hardy had received the remark in silence and with poker face, and I wrote it off as a dud. I later taxed Hardy with this habit ; on which he replied : " Well, what is one to do, is one always to be saying ' damned good ' ? " To which the answer is ' yes '.]

I end with the joke of my own that gives me most pleasure to recall. Veblen was giving a course of 3 lectures on ' Geometry of Paths '. At the end of one lecture the paths had miraculously worked themselves into the form

$$\frac{x-a}{l} = \frac{y-b}{m} = \frac{z-c}{n} = \frac{t-d}{p} \; .$$

He then broke off to make an announcement about what was to follow, ending with the words " I am acting as my own John the Baptist ". With what meaning I do not now recall (certainly not mine), but I was able to seize the Heaven-sent opportunity of saying " Having made your own paths straight ".

⋆ The Zoo

§ 16. The domain obtained by removing an infinity of shaded sectors as in Fig. 10 has very important applications in function-theory (too high-brow to mention here). It is commonly called the amoeba or the star-fish domain.

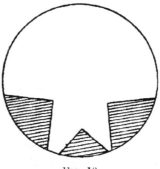

Fig. 10

The snake. Representing the domain shown in Fig. 11 on a unit circle we have a function $f(z)$ that takes some values twice (those in the twice covered region), but for which f'

Fig. 11

never vanishes. (The fallacy that f' must vanish is absurdly common—doubtless an effect of too steady a diet of algebraic function-theory, in which all sheets of the Riemann surfaces are alike and extend over the whole plane.)

45

The crocodile (Fig. 12). The teeth overlap and have a total length just infinite. If the domain is represented on a unit circle we have an example of a function $f(z)=\Sigma c_n z^n$ in which

FIG 12

the real part $U(\theta)$ of $f(e^{i\theta})$ is of bounded variation, and the imaginary part $V(\theta)$ is as nearly so as we like. On the other hand

$$\Sigma|c_n|=\int_0^1(\Sigma_n|c_n|\rho^{n-1})d\rho\geqslant\int_0^1|f'(\rho)|d\rho,$$

and the last integral is the length of the image of the radius vector $(0, 1)$ of the z-circle. This image, however, is some path winding between the teeth to the nose, and has infinite length. Hence $\Sigma|c_n|$ is divergent.

If both U and V are of bounded variation it is a known theorem that the series is convergent. The crocodile shows

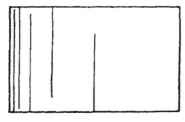

FIG. 13

that the result is best possible, a question I had been asked (by Prof. L. C. Young) to decide. When returning to Cambridge along the Coton footpath the ' hippopotamus ' (Fig. 13, a well-known[1] character in the theory of ' prime-

[1] So well-known, in fact, that my artist does not feel he can take liberties with him.

ends ', but only now baptised in imitation of the crocodile) flashed into my mind from nowhere. He did not quite do the trick (or so I thought), but a couple of hundred yards on he switched to a crocodile.

The hedgehog. Suppose a topological transformation T is such that for each point P of the plane T^nP *ultimately* (i.e. for $n > n_0(P)$) gets into a bounded domain $\varDelta$ *and stays there*. Let $\varDelta_+$ be $\varDelta$ slightly enlarged (i.e. the closure $\bar{\varDelta}$ of $\varDelta$ is contained in $\varDelta_+$). Let $\bar{D}$ be any closed bounded domain. Is it the case that T^nP converges *uniformly* into $\varDelta_+$ for all

FIG. 14

$\varGamma$ of $\bar{D}$ (i.e. $T^n\bar{D} \subset \varDelta_+$ for $n > n_0(\bar{D})$) ? Everyone's first guess is yes (and the corresponding thing is true in 1 dimensions), but the answer is in fact no. For this Miss Cartwright and I found the example of Fig. 14. (There are an infinity of spines running to L, L' as limit points.) Consider a T which leaves the hedgehog (the figure of full lines) invariant as a whole, but transforms each spine into the next one to the right, and further imposes a general contraction of outside points towards the boundary of the hedgehog. $\varDelta$ is the domain bounded by the dotted line, $\varDelta_+$ is $\varDelta$ arbitrarily little enlarged. While T^nP is ultimately inside $\varDelta$ for each P, the tip of a spine near L requires a large n for T^nP to get finally back into $\varDelta_+$.

We later found a much simpler example, Fig. 15, in which u, s, c are respectively totally unstable, stable, and saddle-

point (col) fixed points of the T, and the lines of the figure
are invariant, as wholes, under T. $\varDelta$ is the domain enclosed
by the dotted line. For any P T^nP ultimately stays in $\varDelta$,
but points near u, or again points near the line uc, take

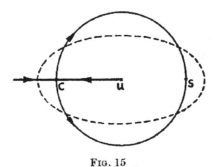

Fɪɢ. 15

arbitrarily long over ending up in $\varDelta_+$. This T, however,
leaves a whole area invariant, and the example does not
cover the important class of T's for which every bounded
area shrinks to zero area under iteration of T. The hedgehog does cover this if his body area is reduced to zero ; he
is not debunked, only disinflated.★

Ballistics

§ 17. '*The rifleman's problem.*' Should the t.e. ϕ (tangent elevation, i e. elevation above the line of sight of a target) for a given range be increased or decreased if the target is slightly above the horizontal ? The answer is probably not intuitive ; but it *is* intuitive that there is a decrease for a target below the horizontal, so the rate of increase with the angle of sight a is presumably positive, and we infer an increase for the original question. For moderate ranges ϕ tends to 0 as a tends to $\frac{1}{2}\pi$, so the initial increase later becomes a decrease. The upshot is that it is a reasonably good approximation to keep ϕ constant for all small positive a[1], this principle is called 'the rigidity of the trajectory'.

The professional (rifleman) believes in the initial increase ; he feels unhappy in firing uphill (and happy firing down). 'The bullet has to pull against the collar.' It is arguable that he is right ; on the one hand the pull is there , on the other the correction that leads ultimately to a decrease is only second order near the horizontal.

In vacuo the height H of a trajectory with horizontal target is $\frac{1}{8}gT'^2(=4T^2)$, where T is the time of flight This happens to be a pretty good approximation over all sorts of guns and all sorts of elevations (even vertical ones).

Suppose we accept these two principles as absolute instead of approximate. Then a curiously ingenious argument becomes possible to arrive at the *position* of the vertex

---

[1] The approximation is improved by the diminishing density of the air upwards. Details are easily worked out for trajectories *in vacuo* ; the *relative* behaviour of actual ones is not very different (and in any case tends to the *in vacuo* behaviour as $\phi \rightarrow 0$)

of a trajectory, given only the range table. * The range
table gives in effect any two of R (range), ϕ (elevation), and
T (time of flight, with $H=4T^2$ linked with it) as functions of
the third.   In Fig. 16 we have, for a given ϕ,

$$\theta+a=\phi,\; r=R(\theta),\; H=4T^2,\; \sin a=H/r,$$

whence

$$R(\theta)\sin(\phi-\theta)=4T^2(\phi),$$

from which a root $\theta(\phi)$ can be found by trial and error, and
thence a and ON.*

My personal contact with this was odd.   On a night not
long before I went to the Ballistic Office (about Dec., 1915)
I was orderly officer for a large Artillery camp with many

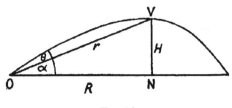

Fig. 16

senior officers (but no professional ballisticians).   Lying on
the office table was the above figure and enough symbols
to show what it was about.   A day or so afterwards a Colonel
asked me whether it was possible to find the position of V.
I gravely reproduced the argument, and as it was new to
him it amused me to say no more.   (I never discovered its
source.)

§ 18.   *Rockets.*   The trajectory of a particle under gravity
and a constant force is an old toy of particle dynamics.
Theoretically the trajectory cannot be started from rest
except vertically.   (With a non-vertical start the initial
curvature is infinite.)

What curves have elegant (*a*) shapes, (*b*) equations ?
A bomb-trajectory has approximately an equation

$$e^{-y}=k \cos x.$$

I heard an account of the battle of the Falkland Islands
(early in the 1914 war) from an officer who was there. The
German ships were destroyed at extreme range, but it took
a long time and salvos were continually falling 100 yards to
the left. The effect of the rotation of the earth is similar to
' drift ' and was similarly incorporated in the gun-sights.
But this involved the tacit assumption that Naval battles
take place round about latitude 50° N. The double difference
for 50° S. and extreme range is of the order of 100 yards.

* § 19. Suppose a particle is projected vertically down-
wards in a medium whose density ρ increases with the depth
y like $1/(1-\lambda y)$, and whose resistance varies as ρv^2, so that
the deceleration due to air resistance is $\mu v^2/(1-\lambda y)$. If now
we have $\mu=\lambda$, then, whatever the initial velocity, *the motion
is simple harmonic* (so long as it lasts ; the bottom end of
the amplitude occurs where the density becomes infinite).
Various attempts of mine to set this in examinations failed.
I had hoped to draw the criticism of ' unreality ', to which
there is the following reply. In 1917-18, a range table was
called for, for the first time, and quickly, for a gun in
an aeroplane flying at a fixed height, to fire in all directions.
A method existed, based on numerical calculation of the
vertically upward and vertically downward trajectories. It
happened that within the permissible limits of accuracy
the values of λ and μ could be faked to make $\lambda=\mu$ (and
$\rho=(1-\lambda y)^{-1}$ was a sufficiently accurate density law). The
downward trajectory could accordingly be read off from a
table of sines, and the range table was in fact made in this
way (in about two-thirds [1] the time it would otherwise have
taken).

---

[1] I *ought* to write $\frac{2}{3}$, but here courage fails me.

§ 20.   I do not deny that the example just given is slightly
disreputable ; here is a more respectable one. For any
' property ' of a trajectory in an atmosphere of varying
density, say the property of having range R for given
elevation (and fixed ' gun ' [1]), there is an ' equivalent
homogeneous atmosphere ' (in which the R for the given ϕ
is the same as in the actual atmosphere , it varies of course
with ϕ) ; this is expressed by a fraction c, the equivalent
constant density being that at height ch, where h is the
greatest height in the trajectory. Now it is always the case,
in any such problem, that in the limit as the length of the
trajectory tends to 0 c is a pure number, independent of the
law of resistance and the rate of variation of density.   In
the particular problem referred to the limiting value is
$c = \frac{3}{5}$. (c varies with the problem and is, e.g. $\frac{2}{5}$ for ' time of
flight given ϕ '.   To establish these results from first
principles requires rather heavy calculations, but these can
be eased by the general knowledge that the limit must be a
pure number.)   The ' average height ' in any ordinary sense
being $\frac{2}{3}h$, this is a mild subtlety (the Office would not believe
it until they had made a numerical experiment, after which
they believed any result guaranteed by theory).   ▬

It is as intuitive as anything can be that, whatever the
' property ', c cannot be outside the range $(0, 1)$: how does
the reader react to the possibility of $c = 0$ or 1 ?

As a matter of fact there exists a very simple (and practically important) case in which $c = 0$: the problem is ' time
of flight on a given inclined plane given the elevation '.

The height h being here only first order (in the flat trajectory it is second order), the calculations are simpler. If we
use the principle that c is independent of the law of resistance
and the rate of variation (the paradox is in any case fully
alive in the limiting case) we can simplify as follows. With
gravity and initial velocity normalized to 1 we may suppose
the retardation to be of the form $\mu(1 - \lambda y)v$, *where μ is small.*

---

[1] A ' gun ' is an ordered pair of constants, (C, V).

Let ϕ be the t.e., a the angle of the inclined plane (Fig. 17). The actual trajectory is the solution of

$$\ddot{x} = -\mu(1-\lambda y)\dot{x}, \quad \ddot{y} = -1-\mu(1-\lambda y)\dot{y},$$

with initial values $\dot{x}_0 = \cos(\phi+a)$, $\dot{y}_0 = \sin(\phi+a)$. The time τ at which $y = x \tan a$ is to be equated to the corresponding time with $\lambda = 0$ and $\mu' = (1-ch)\mu$ for μ. We are to take the

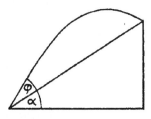

Fig. 17

limit as ϕ (or τ) and μ tend to 0 ($\lambda \to 0$ is not necessary) ; this means *inter alia* that we can ignore all terms involving μ^2 Then approximately

$$\dddot{x} = \lambda\mu x\dot{y}, \quad x^{(4)} = -\lambda\mu\dot{x}, \quad x^{(5)} = 0 \; ;$$

$$\dddot{y} = \mu(1-\lambda y) + \lambda\mu\dot{y}^2, \quad y^{(4)} = -\lambda\mu\ddot{y} + 2\lambda\mu\dot{y}\ddot{y} = -3\lambda\mu\dot{y}, \quad y^{(5)} = 0.$$

At time τ we have, writing γ, σ for $\cos(\phi+a)$, $\sin(\phi+a)$,

$$\gamma \tan a = \frac{y}{x/\gamma} = \sum_1^4 y_0^{(n)} \frac{\tau^n}{n!} \Big/ \sum_1^4 \frac{x_0^{(n)}}{\gamma} \frac{\tau^n}{n!}$$

$$= \{\sigma - \tfrac{1}{2}(1+\mu\sigma)\tau + \tfrac{1}{6}(\lambda\mu\sigma^2+\mu)\tau^2 - \tfrac{3}{24}\lambda\mu\sigma\tau^3\}/\{1 - \tfrac{1}{2}\mu\tau + \tfrac{1}{6}\lambda\mu\sigma\tau^2 - \tfrac{1}{24}\lambda\mu\tau^3\}$$

$$= \sigma - \tfrac{1}{2}\tau - \tfrac{1}{12}\mu\tau^2 + O(\tau^4),$$

by straightforward calculation, ignoring μ^2 : note that there is no term in τ^3.

The right hand side is to be equal to

$$\sigma - \tfrac{1}{2}\tau - \tfrac{1}{12}\mu(1-c\sigma\tau)\tau^2 + O(\tau^4) \; ;$$

hence $c = O(\tau)$ and $c = 0$ in the limit *

The Dilemma of Probability Theory

There is a solid body of propositions of the theory, and no one dreams of doubting their practical applicability. If, for example, a card is drawn 1300 times at random from a (whole) ordinary pack we should be surprised if the number of aces differed greatly from 100, and we believe the more refined statements that it is about an even chance that the number will lie between 94 and 106 inclusive, and that it is one of less than 1 in 10^6 that it will lie outside the range 50 to 150. To avoid possible misunderstanding I begin with a certain distinction. ' The probability of drawing an ace is $\frac{1}{13}$; the probability of drawing an ace twice running is $(\frac{1}{13})^2$.' Such statements, and most of the ' probability ' one meets in algebra text-books, are effectively pure mathematics ; the underlying conventions about ' equal likelihood ' are so inevitable as to be made tacitly, and the subject matter reduces to ' permutations and combinations '. This side of probability theory will not concern us. The earlier statements are very different ; they assert about the real world that such and such events will happen with such and such a probability ; they intend this in the common-sense meaning, and do not intend to say, e.g. that of the 52^{1300} ways of drawing 1300 cards a certain proportion (near $\frac{1}{2}$) contain from 94 to 106 aces. The question now is about the foundations of the subject.

Mathematics (by which I shall mean pure mathematics) has no grip on the real world ; if probability is to deal with the real world it must contain elements outside mathematics ; the *meaning* of ' probability ' must relate to the real world, and there must be one or more ' primitive ' propositions about the real world, from which we can then proceed deductively (i.e. mathematically). We will suppose

54

(as we may by lumping several primitive propositions together) that there is just one primitive proposition, the 'probability axiom', and we will call it A for short. Although it has got to be *true*, A is by the nature of the case incapable of deductive proof, for the sufficient reason that it is about the real world (other sorts of 'justification' I shall consider later).

There are 2 schools. One, which I will call mathematical, stays inside mathematics, with results that I shall consider later. We will begin with the other school, which I will call philosophical. This attacks directly the 'real' probability problem ; what are the axiom A and the meaning of 'probability' to be, and how can we justify A ? It will be instructive to consider the attempt called the 'frequency theory'. It is natural to believe that if (with the natural reservations) an act like throwing a die is repeated n times the proportion of 6's will, *with certainty*, tend to a limit, p say, as $n \rightarrow \infty$. (Attempts are made to sublimate the limit into some Pickwickian sense—'limit' in inverted commas. But either you *mean* the ordinary limit, or else you have the problem of explaining how 'limit' behaves, and you are no further. You do not make an illegitimate conception legitimate by putting it into inverted commas.) If we take this proposition as ' A ' we can at least settle off-hand the other problem, of the *meaning* of probability ; we define its measure for the event in question to be the number p. But for the rest this A takes us nowhere. Suppose we throw 1000 times and wish to know what to expect. Is 1000 large enough for the convergence to have got under way, and how far ? A does not say. We have, then, to add to it something about the rate of convergence. Now an A cannot assert a *certainty* about a particular number n of throws, such as 'the proportion of 6's will *certainly* be within $p \pm \epsilon$ for large enough n (the largeness depending on ϵ) '. It can only say 'the proportion will lie between $p \pm \epsilon$ *with at least such and such probability (depending on ϵ and n_0) whenever $n > n_0$* '. The vicious circle is apparent. We have not merely failed to *justify* a workable A ; we have failed even to *state* one which would work if its truth were granted. It is generally agreed that the frequency theory won't work. But whatever the theory it is clear that the vicious circle is very deep-seated : certainty being impossible, whatever A is made to state can only be in terms of ' probability '. One is tempted to the extreme rashness of saying that the problem is insoluble (within our current conceptions). More sophisticated attempts than the frequency theory have been made, but they fail in the same sort of way.

I said above that an A is inherently incapable of deductive proof. But it is also incapable of inductive proof. If inductive evidence is offered ' in support ' we have only to ask *why* it supports (i.e. gives probability to) A. Justification of a proposition (as opposed to an axiom) can be given only in terms of an earlier proposition or else of an axiom ; justification of a *first* proposition, therefore, only in terms of an axiom. Now any answer to the question ' why ' above is a ' first ' proposition , but the only axiom there is to appeal to is A itself (or part of it), and it is A we are trying to justify. So much for the philosophical school.

The mathematical school develops the theory of a universe of ideal ' events ' E and a function $p(E)$ which has the E's as arguments. Postulates [1] are made about the E's and the function p ; unlike an axiom A, these are not true or false (or even meaningful), but are strictly parallel to the ' axioms ' of modern geometry. The development of the logical consequence of the postulates is a branch of pure mathematics, though the postulates are naturally designed to yield a ' model ' of the accepted body of probability theory. This is in many ways a desirable development . the postulates are chosen to be a minimal set yielding the model theory, and any philosophical discussion can concentrate on them.

---

[1] These are generally called ' axioms ', but I am using ' axiom' in another sense.

Some of the remoter parts of the ordinary theory (e.g. inverse probability) are philosophically controversial , these can be separated from the rest in the model by a corresponding separation of postulates. The purely technical influence of the method on the ordinary theory is also far from negligible ; this is a usual result in mathematics of ' axiomatizing ' a subject. (Incidentally the most natural technical approach is to work with quite general ' additive sets ', with the result that the aspiring reader finds he is expected to know the theory of the Lebesgue integral. He is sometimes shocked at this, but it is entirely natural.)

We come finally, however, to the relation of the ideal theory to the real world, or ' real ' probability. If he is consistent a man of the mathematical school washes his hands of applications. To some one who wants them he would say that the ideal system runs parallel to the usual theory : ' If this is what you want, try it : it is not my business to justify application of the system ; that can only be done by philosophizing , I am a mathematician '. In practice he is apt to say : ' try this ; if it works that will justify it '. But now he is not merely philosophizing; he is committing the characteristic fallacy. Inductive experience that the system works is not evidence.

From Fermat's Last Theorem to the Abolition of Capital Punishment [1]

It is a platitude that pure mathematics can have unexpected consequences and affect even daily life. Could
there be a chain of ideas such as the title suggests ? I think
so, with some give and take ; I propose to imagine at one or
two points slight accidental changes in the course of mathematical history. The amateur should perhaps be warned
that the thesis takes some time to get under way, but moves
rapidly at the end ; I hope he may be persuaded to stay the
earlier course (which incidentally is concerned with ideas of
great mathematical importance).

The theory of numbers is particularly liable to the
accusation that some of its problems may be the wrong sort
of questions to ask. I do not myself think the danger is
serious ; either a reasonable amount of concentration leads
to new ideas or methods of obvious interest, or else one just
leaves the problem alone. 'Perfect numbers' certainly
never did any good, but then they never did any particular
harm. F.L.T. is a provocative case ; it bears every outward
sign of a 'wrong question' (and is a negative theorem at
that) ; yet work on it, as we know, led to the important
mathematical conception of 'ideals'. This is the first link
in my chain of ideas.

The intensive study of F L T. soon revealed that to gain
deeper insight it is necessary to *generalize* the theorem [2] ;
the x, y, z of the 'impossible' $x^p + y^p = z^p$ were generalized

---

[1] I gave the substance of this in a paper at Liverpool about 1929

F.L T. asserts that for an integer n greater than 2 the equation
$x^n + y^n = z^n$ is impossible in integers x, y, z all different from 0. It is
enough to settle the special case in which n is a prime p. Its truth remains
undecided.

[2] And so to attack an apparently more difficult problem !

from being ordinary integers to being integers of the ' field '
of the equation $\zeta^p + 1 = 0$. If a is a root (other than -1)
of this equation, then the integers of the field are, nearly
enough for present purposes, all the numbers of the form
$m_0 + m_1a + \cdots + m_{p-2}a^{p-1}$, where the m's are ' ordinary ' integers (of either sign). The idea of the divisibility of a field
integer a by another, b, is simple enough, a is divisible by b if
$a = bc$, where c is a field integer. Again, a field prime is a field
integer with no ' proper ' divisor, that is, is divisible only by
itself and by the field ' unities ' (generalizations of ' 1 ', they
divide all field integers). Any (field) integer can further be
resolved into prime ' factors '. But now a new situation
develops with the fields of some (indeed most) p's, resolu-
tion into prime factors is not (as it is for ordinary integers)
always unique. ' Ideals ' are called in to restore uniqueness
of factorization.[1]

New entities like ideals generally begin as a ' postulation ',
being later put on a rigorous basis by the ' construction ' of
an entity which behaves as desired.[2] The easiest course at
this point is to give at once Dedekind's construction, and go
on from there. If a, β, , κ are any finite set of field
integers, consider the class of all numbers (they are field
integers) of the form $ma + \cdots + k\kappa$, where $m, \ldots, k$ are
ordinary integers , a number of the class is ' counted only
once ' if there is overlapping. The class, which is completely
determined by the set $a, . , \kappa$, is denoted by $(a, . , \kappa)$ and
is called an ' ideal '. Let us now go back to the ' field ' of
ordinary integers and see what an ' ideal ' becomes in that
special case. The (ordinary) integers $a, .., \kappa$ have a
' greatest common divisor ' d (and this fact is the basis of
' unique factorization '— Euclid makes it so in his proof, and
this is the ' right ' proof, though text-books often give
another). The class of numbers $ma + \cdots + k\kappa$, when the

---

[1] For integers of the field of a general algebraic equation
$a_0 + a_1\zeta + \cdots + a^n\zeta^n = 0$, where the a's are ordinary integers.

[2] Other instances complex numbers, points at infinity ; non-
Euclidean geometry.

extensive overlapping is ignored, is easily seen to be identical with the class of numbers nd (n taking all ordinary integral values) ; the ideal $(a, \ldots, \kappa)$ is identical with the ideal (d). An ideal in the general field which is of the form (a) (a being a field integer) is called a 'principal ideal' : the field of ordinary integers has, then, the property that *all* its ideals are principal. Suppose next that a, b are ordinary integers and that b divides a, e.g. let $a=6$, $b=3$. Then (a) is the class of all multiples of 6, (b) the class of all multiples of 3, and *the class (a) is contained in the class (b)*. Conversely this can happen only if a *is* divisible by b. Thus ' b divides a ' and ' (a) is contained in (b) ' are exactly equivalent. Now the set of entities (a) is in exact correspondence with the set of entities a (without the brackets) ; we can take the ideals (a) for raw material instead of the integers a, and interpret ' (b) divides (a) ' as meaning ' (a) is contained in (b) '. The theory of the bracketed entities runs parallel to that of the unbracketed ones, and is a mere 'translation' of the latter. Return to the general field. The integer a gets replaced by (a), but all ideals are no longer principal, the totality of *all* ideals is taken for the raw material, and divisibility of a 1st ideal by a 2nd (so far not defined) is taken to mean the containing of the 1st ideal (qua class) in the 2nd. Suppose now, denoting ideals by Clarendon type, that $\mathbf{a}, \ldots, \mathbf{k}$ are a finite set of ideals. There is then an ideal $\mathbf{d}$ whose class contains each of the classes of $\mathbf{a}$, ., $\mathbf{k}$, and which is the smallest of this kind [1] : $\mathbf{d}$ functions as a 'greatest common divisor' of $\mathbf{a}$, , $\mathbf{k}$. After this we arrive without difficulty (and much as in the 'ordinary' case) at the key proposition that every ideal can be factorized uniquely into 'prime ideals'. Since this theory 'reduces' to the 'ordinary' theory in the special case of 'ordinary' integers it is a genuine *generalization* of the latter, and may legitimately be said to 'restore' unique factorization.

---

[1] If $\mathbf{a} = (a_1, \beta_1, \ . \ , \kappa_1), \ldots \mathbf{k} = (a_n, \beta_n, \ldots, \kappa_n)$, then actually
$$\mathbf{d} = (a_1, \quad , \kappa_1, \ . \ , a_n, . \ . \ , \kappa_n).$$

I feel that ideals ' ought ' to have been created first, and to have suggested the famous ' Dedekind section ' definition of ' real numbers ', but though it was a near thing the facts are otherwise.[1] We will, however, suppose history modified.

In a Dedekind section *all* rational numbers fall into one of two classes, L and R,[2] every member of L being to the left of (i.e. less than) every member of R (and for definiteness L has no greatest member—R may or may not happen to have one). The totality of all possible ' sections of the rationals ' provides a set of entities with the properties we wish the continuum of ' real numbers ' to have, and real numbers become properly founded.

What exactly does ' section ' (' Schnitt ') mean ? After the class definition of the ideal it would seem natural— almost inevitable—to define it, and the real number also, to *be* the class L (of course R would do equally well). Thus the real number 2 *is* the class of rationals r composed of the negative ones together with the non-negative ones satisfying $r^2 < 2$. It is reasonable to take the step for granted and call this Dedekind's definition. The actual circumstances are very strange. For Dedekind the Schnitt is an act of cutting, not the thing cut off ; he ' postulates ' a ' real number ' to do the cutting and is not entirely happy about it (and the modern student is much happier with the *class*) : as Bertrand Russell says, the method of postulation has many advantages, which are the same as those of theft over honest toil. Incidentally, on a point of linguistics, both ' Schnitt ' and ' section ' are ambiguous and can mean either the act of

[1] Publication was more or less contemporaneous (and the later idea was available for revision of the earlier), but the ' section ', published 1872 (' Was sind usw. ? '), originated in 1858

[2] The letters L, R, for which a generation of students is rightly grateful, were introduced by me In the first edition of *Pure Mathematics* they are T, U. The latest editions have handsome references to me, but when I told Hardy he should acknowledge this contribution (which he had forgotten) he refused on the ground that it would be insulting to mention anything so minor. (The familiar response of the oppressor : what the victim wants is not in his own best interests)

cutting or the thing cut off : it is a case in which a mis-reading could have constituted an advance.

These two ' class ' definitions (ideal and real number) have no parallel since about 350 B.C. Eudoxus's (Fifth book of Euclid) definition of ' equal ratio ' (of incommensurables) is in fact very near the Dedekind section (Eudoxus's equal $a : b$ and $c : d$ correspond each to the same ' class of rationals m/n ' ; the class of m/n's for which $ma<nb$ is identical with that for which $mc<nd$).

Turn now to another question: what is meant by a ' function ' ? I will digress (though with a purpose) to give some extracts from Forsyth's *Theory of Functions of a Complex Variable*; this is intended to make things easy for the beginner. (It was out of date when written (1893), but this is the sort of thing my generation had to go through. The fact that ' regularity ' of a function of a complex variable is being explained at the same time adds unfairly to the general horror, but I should be sorry to deprive my readers of an intellectual treat. In case they feel they have had enough before the end they may note that the passage ends on p. 64, l. 24.)

' All ordinary operations effected on a complex variable lead, as already remarked, to other complex variables ; and any definite quantity, thus obtained by operations on z, is necessarily a function of z.

But if a complex variable w is given as a complex function of x and y without any indication of its source, the question as to whether w is or is not a function of z requires a consideration of the general idea of functionality.

It is convenient to postulate $u+iv$ as a form of the complex variable, where u and v are real. Since w is initially un-restricted in variation, we may so far regard the quantities u and v as independent and therefore as any functions of x and y, the elements involved in z. But more explicit expressions for these functions are neither assigned nor supposed.

The earliest occurrence of the idea of functionality is in connection with functions of real variables ; and then it is coextensive with the idea of dependence. Thus, if the value of X depends on that of x and on no other variable magnitude, it is customary to regard X as a function of x , and there is usually an implication that X is derived from x by some series of operations.

A detailed knowledge of z determines x and y uniquely ; hence the values of u and v may be considered as known and therefore also w. Thus the value of w is dependent on that of z, and is independent of the values of variables unconnected with z , therefore, with the foregoing view of functionality, w is a function of z.

It is, however, consistent with that view to regard as a complex function of the two independent elements from which z is constituted ; and we are then led merely to the consideration of functions of two real independent variables with (possibly) imaginary coefficients.

Both of these aspects of the dependence of w on z require that z be regarded as a composite quantity involving two independent elements which can be considered separately. Our purpose, however, is to regard z as the most general form of algebraic variable and therefore as an irresoluble entity ; so that, as this preliminary requirement in regard to z is unsatisfied, neither of these aspects can be adopted.

Suppose that w is regarded as a function of z in the sense that it can be constructed by definite operations on z regarded as an irresoluble magnitude, the quantities u and v arising subsequently to these operations by the separation of the real and imaginary parts when z is replaced by $x+iy$. It is thereby assumed that one series of operations is sufficient for the simultaneous construction of u and v, instead of one series for u and another series for v as in the general case of a complex function [above]. If this assumption be justified by the same forms resulting from the two different methods of construction, it follows that the two series of operations, which lead in the general case to u and to v, must be equivalent to the single series and must therefore be connected by conditions ; that is, u and v as functions of x and y must have their functional forms related :

$$(1) \qquad \frac{\partial w}{\partial x} = \frac{1}{i}\frac{\partial w}{\partial y} = \frac{dw}{dy}$$

$$(2) \qquad -\frac{\partial v}{\partial x} = \frac{\partial u}{\partial y}, \quad \frac{\partial u}{\partial x} = \frac{\partial v}{\partial y}.$$

These are necessary . . . and sufficient . . . relations between the functional forms of u and v.

The preceding determination of the necessary and sufficient conditions of functional dependence is based on the existence of a functional form , and yet that form is not essential, for, as already remarked, it disappears from the equations of condition Now the postulation of such a form is equivalent to an assumption that the function can be numerically calculated for each particular value of the independent variable, though the immediate expression of the assumption has disappeared in the present case. Experience of functions of real variables shews that it is often more convenient to use their properties than to possess their numerical values. This experience is confirmed by what has preceded. The essential conditions of functional dependence are the equations (1) . . . .'

Nowadays, of course, a function $y = y(x)$ means that there is a class of ' arguments ' x, and to each x there is assigned 1 and only 1 ' value ' y. After some trivial explanations (or none ?) we can be balder still, and say that a function is a class C of pairs (x, y) (order within the bracket counting), C being subject (only) to the condition that the x's of different pairs are different. (And a ' relation ', ' x has the relation R to y ', reduces *simply* to a class, which may be any class whatever, of ordered pairs.) Nowadays, again, the x's may be any sort of entities whatever, and so may the y's (e.g. classes, propositions). If we *want* to consider well-behaved functions, e.g. ' continuous ' ones of a real variable, or Forsyth's $f(z)$, we *define* what being such a function means (2 lines for Forsyth's function), and ' consider ' the class of functions so restricted. That is all. This clear daylight is now a matter of course, but it replaces an obscurity as of midnight.[1] The main step was taken by Dirichlet in 1837 (for functions of a real variable, the argument class consisting of some or all real numbers and the value class confined to real numbers). The complete emancipation of e.g. propositional functions belongs to the 1920's.

Suppose now, again to imagine a modified history, that the way out into daylight had been slightly delayed and pointed (as it easily might have been) by the success of Dedekind's ideas. I will treat the idea of function, then, as derived from the Fermat theorem. (If this is rejected ' abolition ' will be related instead to Fourier series or the differential equations of heat conduction.)

Consider now a function in which the argument class consists of the moments t of (historical) time and the value $f(t)$ for argument t is a state of the Universe (described in sufficient detail to record any happening of interest to anybody). If t_0 is the present date, $f(t)$, for $t < t_0$, is a description, or dictionary, of what *has* happened. Suppose now the dictionary transported back to an earlier time τ ; then it contains a prediction of what is going to happen between times τ and t_0. This argument is clearly *relevant* to the issue of determination versus free-will and could reinforce any existing doubts. Doubts about free-will bear on the problem of moral responsibility and so (rightly or wrongly) on the problem of punishment. Wilder ideas have influenced vigorous reformers.

---

[1] The trouble was, of course, an obstinate feeling at the back of the mind that the value of a function ' ought ' to be got from the argument by ' a series of operations '.

A Mathematical Education

It is *my* education. It illustrates conditions before 1907, but has some oddities of its own.

I am sure that I do not suffer from the weakness of false modesty, and to begin with I do not mind saying that I was precocious : as a matter of fact precocity in a mathematician has no particular significance one way or the other, and there are plenty of examples both ways ; I happen to belong to the precocious class.

Born June 9, 1885, I was in South Africa from 1892 to 1900 , I left the Cape University at the age of 14, and after 2 or 3 months went to England to go to St. Paul's School, where I was taught for 3 years by F. S. Macaulay. My knowledge then was slight by modern standards ; the first 6 books of Euclid, a little algebra, trigonometry up to solution of triangles. During my 3 years at St. Paul's I worked intensively ; seriously overworked indeed, partly because it was a period of severe mental depression.

The tradition of teaching (derived ultimately from Cambridge) was to study ' lower ' methods intensively before going on to ' higher ' ones ; thus analytical methods in geometry were taken late, and calculus very late. And each book was more or less finished before we went on to the next. The accepted sequence of books was . Smith's *Algebra* ; Loney's *Trigonometry* ; *Geometrical Conics* (in a very stiff book of Macaulay's own : metrical properties of the parabola, for instance, gave scope for infinite virtuosity) ; Loney's *Statics and Dynamics*, without calculus ; C. Smith's *Analytical Conics* ; Edward's *Differential Calculus* ; Williamson's *Integral Calculus* ; Besant's *Hydrostatics*. These were annotated by Macaulay and provided with revision papers at intervals. · Beyond this point the order

66

could be varied to suit individual tastes. My sequence, I think, was : Casey's *Sequel to Euclid* ; Chrystal's *Algebra II* ; Salmon's *Conics*; Hobson's *Trigonometry* (2nd edition, 1897); Routh's *Dynamics of a Particle* (a book of more than 400 pages and containing some remarkably highbrow excursions towards the end) ; Routh's *Rigid Dynamics* ; Spherical Trigonometry (in every possible detail) ; Murray's *Differential Equations* ; Smith's *Solid Geometry* ; Burnside and Panton's *Theory of Equations* ; Minchin's *Statics* (omitting elasticity, but including attractions, with spherical harmonics, and—of course —an exhaustive treatment of the attractions of ellipsoids).

I had read nearly all of this before the Entrance Scholarship Examination of December 1902. (I was expected to do well, but I found the papers difficult and got only a Minor Scholarship at Trinity.[1] I had had a severe attack of influenza some weeks before, and though I did not feel mentally unfit I certainly must have been.) We were not overtaught and there were no oral lessons, and while anyone *could* go to Macaulay in a difficulty it was on the whole not done. We went up, of course, with paper work at intervals, at first from examples marked by him in the current book, later from our own selections. (There was a weekly problem paper from Wolstenholme's collection, set at one time by him, later by the head boy, who was myself in my last year ; if we all failed at a problem it became Macaulay's duty to perform at sight at the blackboard.) The class were encouraged to go to seniors for help, I should say to the great benefit of all concerned. Work directly for the Scholarship Examination was confined to a revision in the preceding term. (His academic successes, however, were notorious. In his 25 years at the School there were

---

[1] I remember being horribly put off in the first paper by sitting opposite a man who was rapidly reeling off the questions . I changed my seat for later papers. It must have been Mercer (who was a graduate of Manchester University and was making a fresh start at Cambridge, a not uncommon practice at the time).

I remember also that Cambridge inspired in me an awe equalled by nothing I have felt since.

41 scholarships (34 in Cambridge) and 11 exhibitions ; and in the 20 years available these provided 4 Senior Wranglers, 1 2nd, and 1 4th. My own period was a peak. G. N. Watson, a year my junior at the school and at Cambridge, was also a Senior Wrangler ; incidentally he was fully as precocious as myself. G. R. Blanco-White, a year my senior, was 2nd Wrangler.) Dr. Maxwell Garnett's description of the education as having a University atmosphere is a fair one. Self-reliance being the expected thing we mostly acquired it, and as Macaulay himself did creative work (he became an F.R.S. in 1928) we caught something of the feeling that mathematics was a natural activity.

There was nothing much wrong with my education so far and what was wrong was inherent in the system. Ideally I should have learnt analysis from a French Cour d'Analyse instead of from Chrystal and Hobson, but this would have been utterly unconventional. I did not see myself as a pure mathematician (still less as an analyst) until after my Tripos Part I, but I had enough instinctive interest in rigour to make me master the chapters of Chrystal on limits and convergence. The work is rigorous (within reasonable limits), and I really did understand, for instance, uniform convergence, but it is appallingly heavy going. (The 2nd edition of Hobson (1897) was a strange mixture, as Macaulay observed in a marginal note, of careful rigour and astonishing howlers [1], but I had done the ' convergence ' sections in Chrystal.)

From this point (the Scholarship Examination), however,

---

* [1] E.g. the fallacious proof that two power series agreeing in value have identical coefficients On pp 243-4, again, there are remarkable passages. ' If the limit of S_n is infinite, or if it is finite but not definite, the series is not convergent.' ' To show that [the general principle of convergence] is sufficient, denote by R_n the infinite series $a_{n+1}+a_{n+2}+\ldots$, the remainder after n terms, then by making r [in $\sum\limits_{n+1}^{n+r}$] infinite, we see that $|R_n| < \epsilon$ if $n \gtrless m$, hence S has a value between $S_n \pm \epsilon$ [and ϵ is arbitrarily small] ; also S_n being the sum of a number of finite quantities is finite, hence S is finite. Thus $S_{n+r}-S_n$ can be made as small as we please by

I wasted my time, except for rare interludes, for $2\frac{1}{2}$ years (8 months at school, 2 academic years at Cambridge). First the 8 months at school. Rightly enough to begin with, I read Smith's *Solid Geometry* : this did not take long, though I recall that while I followed it easily enough I failed to digest it for examination purposes and did very badly in the questions in the final school examination. The best things to do in applied mathematics would have been the ' water, gas and electricity ' subjects. There was probably no suitable text-book on electricity, but Lamb's *Hydrodynamics* was available. The prolonged study of dynamics for some reason (my own fault) stopped short at only the elements of moving axes. In pure mathematics the ideal would again have been more *Cours d'Analyse*. Instead of such things I spent a long time reading Tait's book on the futile subject of Quaternions. Then occurred one of the interludes : I read Harkness and Morley's *Introduction to the Theory of Analytic Functions* (1898). The correct thing to say would be something about the opening up of infinite horizons and a new spirit of approach to mathematics. The cold facts were quite different. I was indeed greatly struck by individual things [1] and a number of them stuck with me for a long time [2]. But no infinite horizons. I am, as a

---

making n large enough, therefore $\lim S_n = \lim S_{n+r}$, hence the value of S is definite, being independent of the form of n ' [Trivial alterations to abbreviate, punctuation as in the original]* Hobson was a professional analyst when he wrote this it is a case, certainly very extreme, of blind spots and blindly following tradition when writing a text-book—one cannot be reopening questions all the time. I once caught myself in lecture reproducing a very bad test for differentiating under the integral sign, oblivious of the good one I should be using if I were writing a paper.

[1] Much as everyone is struck on first meeting definite integrals by contour integration ; this was in fact one of the things

[2] This led to an incident in my first term at Cambridge Our lecturer on analysis was rather a martinet. On one occasion I know exactly what was coming, having read it in H. and M. : I wrote it all down at speed and looked elaborately out of the window ' Are you not taking this down, Sir ? ' ' I've got it down.' He visibly hesitated whether to ask to see it (I was not then known to be any good), but in the end said ' I beg your pardon.' The class thought I had scored, but for myself I felt that he had, by making me feel a boor.

matter of fact, sceptical about such ' introductions ' : they can seem admirable if you know the subject already, but I don't think they thrill the beginner, at least legitimately ; nothing but the hard technical story is any real good. Incidentally the book is a bit woolly in its account of real numbers ; this was perhaps hardly avoidable in 1898 ; nothing my generation ever came across (at any rate in English) had the sharp bracing precision the student gets today.

On coming up to Cambridge (October 1903) I coached for 2 years (20 months [1]) for Part I of the Tripos with R. A. Herman, contemporary and friend of my father, and the last of the great coaches.[2] The period is gloomy to look back on. If I am to record new things I acquired which were in any sense worth acquiring, they were moving axes in dynamics, hydro-dynamics, and differential geometry (beyond what was in Smith). Also small additions to what I knew already in spherical harmonics and complex variable analysis. Electricity was completely scrappy and I never saw Maxwell's equations.[3] Enthusiasm was touched just twice, by a stimulating course in the first term by A. N. Whitehead on the foundations of mechanics, and by an admirable one on differential geometry given by Herman in his capacity of College lecturer, of which more later. To be in the running for Senior Wrangler one had to spend two-thirds of the time practising how to solve difficult problems against time. I remember that I had then no serious use for lectures, except Herman's ; my note-books show that I attended only about half the time, and in such cases I never looked at the notes again.

[1] One long vacation only.

[2] The reform of 1910 extinguished almost at once the general practice of coaching.

[3] It is fair to say that in 2 years I could not use all the available courses (College or coaching) For completeness I should add that I wasted time on optics and astronomy (*not* worth knowing) and then practically disregarded them.

It used to be claimed that the discipline in ' manipulative skill ' bore later fruit in original work. I should deny this almost absolutely—such skill is very short-winded. My actual experience has been that after a few years nothing remained to show for it all except the knack, which has lasted, of throwing off a set of (modern) Tripos questions both suitable and with the silly little touch of distinction we still feel is called for ; this never bothers me as it does my juniors. (I said ' almost ' absolutely , there could be rare exceptions If Herman had been put on to some of the more elusive elementary inequalities at the right moment I can imagine his anticipating some of the latest and slickest proofs, perhaps even making new discoveries.)

The old Tripos and its vices are dead horses , I will not flog them. I do not claim to have suffered high-souled frustration. I took things as they came ; the game we were playing came easily to me, and I even felt a sort of satis- faction in successful craftsmanship.

My detailed career for the 20 months was as follows. I overworked in my 1st Michaelmas term. On the other hand, I did all but no work in the Lent term (part cause training for the Lent races) ; in consequence I took the Trinity March Scholarship examination [1], for which anyhow it was impossible to prepare, feeling at the top of my form, and reversed my failure in the Entrance by coming out top of the list. In June I took 2nd year Mays and came out top (Mercer not sitting). I got full marks in the Analysis paper, my first contact with a startled Hardy, who had just come on the Trinity staff (and was privately coaching Mercer). In my 2nd year the only academic event was the Tripos (which I took while still 19) : I was bracketed Senior Wrangler with Mercer.

The Mays Analysis paper reminds me of a fatuous experi-

[1] For Senior Scholarships, and open to all (including Entrance Scholars) not already Senior Scholars: it is now abolished,

ment, and I will digress. I lived in Bideford (Devon) and
decided to spend part of the Easter vacation buried at Hart-
land Quay (in superb scenery and the spot in England most
distant from a railway station). The idea was to give up
smoking, concentrate on work in the mornings and late
afternoons, and ' relax ' on poetry and philosophy (Principia
Ethica) in the evenings, fortified by strong coffee. (Incidentally my generation worked mainly at night, and 1 o'clock
was early to go to bed : there was also a monstrous belief
that 8 hours was the minimum a mathematician should work
a day ; the really virtuous man, by cutting down his sleep,
should achieve 10.) My window opened on the sea, which I
used as a waste-paper-basket, and on arrival I ceremonially
threw my pipes and tobacco into it. Next day I relapsed.
The work I got through was very slight, but it consisted in
reading the parts of Whittaker's *Modern Analysis* I did not
already know, and revising, and this is why analysis was at
my fingers' ends in the Mays. The experiment taught me
something of the truth that for serious work one does best
with a background of familiar routine, and that in the
intervals for relaxation one should *be* relaxed. Much could
be said on this theme, but this is not the moment for it :
I will say, however, that for me the thing to avoid, for
doing creative work, is above all Cambridge life, with the
constant bright conversation of the clever, the wrong sort
of mental stimulus, all the goods in the front window.

Something about the M.T.I. examination itself.   It
consisted of 7 papers (' 1st 4 days ') on comparatively
elementary subjects, the riders, however, being quite stiff,
followed a week later by another 7 (' 2nd 4 days '). A pass
on the 1st 4 days qualified for a degree, but the 2nd 4 days
carried double the marks, and since it was impossible to
revise everything the leading candidates concentrated on
the 2nd 4 days[1], in which, moreover, it was generally

---

[1] I did one very bad paper in the first four days, all optics and
astronomy.

possible to find enough questions without preparing all
subjects. The leaders generally came out pretty level on
the 1st 4 days, and the things they used to do I now find
almost incredible. It is a lost world, and except for odd
accidents I cannot remotely guess what questions I did, but
I inherited the, mark sheets of my year (1905) from one of
the examiners. The marks of the leaders in the 1st 4 days,
ignoring the problem paper, were 1350, 1330, 1280, 1230
(the Senior Wranglers 3rd and 4th), followed by 8 more, of
whom the last got 990. Full marks were 1930, and the
papers were of 10 questions, for the most part with stiff
riders. On the problem paper Mercer got 270 out of 760
for 18 *questions* (I got only 180). In one paper I got 177
out of 230 for the riders, and I can remember something of
this. One question was pure book-work about Carnot's
cycle, of which I had not heard. Another was about a
condenser, of which I also had not heard, but I reconstructed
the question from the answer to the rider. My recollection,
however, is that I did *all* that paper apart from Carnot :
the marks I dropped must have been for inaccuracy and my
notoriously slovenly ' style ' [1]. In the 2nd 4 days (ignoring
the problem paper) Mercer and I each got about 2050 out
of 4500 (each about 330 out of 1340 in the 18 question
problem paper). What staggers me most here was a paper
(mixed pure and applied) in which I got practically full
marks for book-work (290 out of 310, apparently I avoided
' slovenliness ' here) *plus* 250 out of 590 for the riders.

The marks of the candidates have a frequency graph not
at all Gaussian ; it is horizontal from the highest point

---

[1] I do not take off marks in examinations for slovenliness as such
(and always protest against examiners' bleatings that ' the numerical
work was slovenly and inaccurate '). Muddled writing in considered work
is of course a heinous crime, but at speed and at examination level it is
trivial Much nonsense used to be talked about this It amuses me to
recall the man, famous for clear thinking emerging in faultless copper-
plate even in examinations, and held up to us as a model In his later
career he wrote more bad, muddled, and completely wrong mathematics
than anyone before or since

onward. Explanations suggest themselves, but oddly enough the graph of a recent Mays examination is roughly Gaussian.

There is only one other question I am sure of having done, and for the following reason. I began on a question on elementary theory of numbers, in which I felt safe in my school days. It did not come out, nor did it on a later attack. I had occasion to fetch more paper ; when passing a desk my eye lit on a heavy mark against the question. The candidate was not one of the leading people, and I half-unconsciously inferred that I was making unnecessarily heavy weather ; the question then came out fairly easily. The perfectly highminded ʼman would no doubt have abstained from further attack ; I wish I had done so, but the offence does not lie very heavily on my conscience.

The M.T. II (1906). This dealt in quite genuine mathematics (and except that the corresponding Part III is now taken in the 3rd instead of a normal 4th year the examination has been much the same ever since the ʼ80's). I wasted a good deal of time, unluckily in some ways, but partly in the ordinary course of trial and error. Pursuing differential geometry, I embarked on Darboux's *Théorie des Surfaces*, and read 3 of the 4 volumes (i e 1 read 1500 pages). It is a beautiful work, but my initial enthusiasm flagged : it was not my subject. In the examination there were several questions on it ; I did them all ; but I could have done them the year before, from Herman's lectures. The rest of my studies were in analysis of a sort. One thing Cambridge made almost inevitable for an analyst ; intensive study of Legendre functions, and all that. Such ' dictionary ' subjects are utterly unsuitable for a good man. It was, however, the more inevitable in that a lecture was provided (by E. W. Hobson ; he later wrote a standard text-book) : I was the sole member of the class. It amuses me to recall that I could get up this kind of thing completely by heart : several questions were set and I wiped the floor with all of them. I attended, also as sole member of the class, a lecture by E. W. Barnes on his current work on double Γ and ζ functions. There was a highly individual lecture by H. F. Baker, on selected points from widely scattered branches of analysis ; this was stimulating but not intended to be pedagogic. I presented the more elementary of the two parts constituting ' Elliptic Functions ' in the Schedule and ' attended ' the course on this by A. Berry. The lectures, however, were at 9 a.m., and I managed to get there only about half the time (working as I did till 2 or 3 in the morning) ; I never read up the notes, nor did I follow the obvious course of reading a text-book (though we depended far more on text-books and less on lectures than now), and I abandoned the subject for examination purposes. The fact is that I had as yet no sort of idea of what was good for me, and, again, I read no complex function theory proper. Having somehow acquired a working knowledge of Analysis I never read seriously any of the *Cours d'Analyse*. Others have put on record how Jordan first opened their eyes to what real mathematics was ; this I missed. But I was also very casual, Picard would certainly have been very good for me. My memory of all this is very hazy and I must have read things I have forgotten. A few weeks before the examination, in the Easter term, I first came across the early volumes of the Borel series, and it was these, in cold fact, that first gave me an authentic thrill : series of positive terms, divergent series, and the volume on integral functions. The first 2 were irrelevant for the examination ; the last I presented officially, but I lost the book, could not conveniently get another copy, and did not prepare it. But now I knew the kind of thing I wanted.

For special reasons I can identify the details about one paper (Friday, June 1, 1906, 9-12), and it interests me, in the light of my later activities, to see what I did *not* then know. There were 6 questions :

    1. Elaborate Legendre functions.

2. Multiplication of series.
3. Discontinuous Riemann integrable function.
4. Reversion of power series (with a specific radius of convergence to be established).
5. Conformal representation of an oval on a half-plane.
6. Elliptic functions (θ-functions from the part of the subject I was not presenting).

In this the only question I was supposed to know about was number 1 (where of course I got full marks at high speed). By the rules of the game this entitled me to fullest possible marks for the whole paper ; but in such cases one was naturally a little nervous about whether the examiners would notice, and this is why I remember everything. I knew something about number 4 unofficially, but not in the precise form given, so my answer was imperfect. About all the rest my ignorance was actual as well as official (though 5 years earlier, at school, I had known number 2).

I was told that I had done very well in the whole examination. I had, however, not yet technically qualified for a degree. In those days a Tripos taken in one's 2nd year did not count at all, and while M.T. II qualified for a degree when taken in one's 4th year it did not do so in one's 3rd. There have always been provisions (Special Graces of the Senate) for dealing with anomalies, however, and I heard about this only by chance.

There were 9 classes, I(1) to III(3). The standard was sometimes preposterous, and the examination went out in 1910 in a blaze of glory. An unusually large and strong field included 6 people afterwards well-known as Professors of mathematics, or an equivalent ; class I division 1 was empty. It was empty also the previous year, and had only 1 member the year before that.

To finish with lectures. In my 4th year there were probably few left for me to go to. A. R. Forsyth (Sadleirian Professor) gave a course on differential equations ; this did not appeal to me. What I did go to were courses by Whitehead on foundations of geometry and on foundations of mathematics, given for the first time. There were 3 or 4 of us in the class and we found them very exciting. (Whitehead had recently been made a Senior College Lecturer at Trinity, with the duty of giving lectures out of the ordinary run. His stock College lectures, except for the one on the principles of mechanics, were solid and unexciting affairs on applied mathematics : a mathematician can have the duty of being dull—Eddington lecturing on Spherical Trigonometry.) I cannot remember going to any other lectures.

My research began, naturally, in the Long Vacation of my 3rd year, 1906. My director of studies (and tutor) E. W. Barnes suggested the subject of integral functions of order 0. The first idea was to find asymptotic formulae for functions with simple given zeros like $a_n = e^n$; the analytic methods he had been using with success for non-zero order were not working. Incidentally this brought me into touch with another famous and important Borel volume, Lindelöf's *Calcul des Résidus*. There were the best of reasons for the method's not working, as appeared later, but the general suggestion was an excellent one , I rather luckily struck oil at once by switching to more ' elementary ' methods, and after that never looked back. The conjecture soon suggested itself that a function of order 0 would, on some large circles, have the property

$$m(r) > (M(r))^{1-\epsilon},$$

where $M(r)$ and $m(r)$ are the maximum and minimum moduli. By my elementary methods, at least, this is quite tough, and it took me probably a couple of months. (The corresponding result for non-zero order is that for order less than $\frac{1}{2}$ $m(r)$ is as large as a positive power of $M(r)$ (on some circles). This I could prove only with $\frac{1}{4}$ for $\frac{1}{2}$, and the full result was proved later by A. Wiman by more ' function-theory ' methods. A. S. Besicovitch, however, has recently revived the elementary method to prove further extensions.) I sent a longish paper (about functions of order 0) to the London Mathematical Society (Jan. 1, 1907). I should omit a good deal today, but it was not too obscurely written, and the $m > M^{1-\epsilon}$ result is quite respectable. It also contains what I believe is the first instance of a certain 'averaging argument'. (One wants to prove that a function $f(x)$ exceeds a suitable lower bound m at *some* point of a range $0 \leqslant x \leqslant 1$, say. Each individual point is intractable but the way out sometimes exists that the average of $f(x)$ over $(0, 1)$ can be shown to exceed an m; then *some* x, though unidentifiable, must make $f(x) > m$.) The referees disagreed, one being violently unfavourable (by the time I learned in later life who he was I had disinterestedly come to think him a bit of an ass). Hardy was appointed as 3rd referee and the paper was duly published. I have not since had trouble with papers, with the single exception that the Cambridge Philosophical Society once rejected (quite wrongly) one written in collaboration with Hardy.

Barnes was now encouraged to suggest a new problem : ' prove the Riemann Hypothesis '. As a matter of fact this heroic suggestion was not without result ; but I must begin by sketching the background of $\zeta(s)$ and prime numbers in 1907, especially so far as I was myself concerned. I had met $\zeta(s)$ in Lindelöf, but there is nothing there about primes, nor had I the faintest idea there was any connexion , for me the R.H. was famous, but only as a problem in integral functions ; and all this took place in the Long Vacation when I had no access to literature, had I suspected there was any. (As for people better instructed, only some had heard of Hadamard's paper, and fewer still knew of de la Vallée Poussin's in a Belgian journal. In any case, the work was considered very sophisticated and outside the main stream of mathematics. The famous paper of Riemann is included in his collected works ; this states the R.H., and the extraordinary, but unproved, ' explicit formula ' for $\pi(x)$; the ' Prime Number Theorem ' is not mentioned, though it is doubtless an easy guess granted the explicit formula. As for Hardy in particular, he told me later that he ' knew ' the P.N.T. had been proved, but he thought by Riemann. All this was transformed at a stroke by the appearance of Landau's book in 1909.)

I remembered the Euler formula $\zeta(s)=\Pi(1-p^{-s})^{-1}$; it was introduced to us at school, as a *joke* (rightly enough, and in excellent taste). (Oddly enough it ıs not in Chrystal's *Algebra* ; but in the ' convergence ' chapter there is an example, with references : $\Sigma f(p)$ is convergent if $\Sigma f(n)/\log n$ is. The n's are however misprınted as p's. Against the resulting false statement I find a note made by me in 1902, query $f(p)=1/p$ I was sure in 1902 that $\Sigma 1/(p\log p)$ converges—it is actually not too big a jump from the Euler product.) In the light of Euler's formula it is natural to study $P(s)=\Sigma p^{-s}$. I soon saw that if the P.N.T. were true ' with error about $\sqrt{x}$ ' the R.H. would follow. Now at that time, and for anyone unacquainted with the literature, there was no reason to expect any devılment in the primes And the $\sqrt{x}$ seems entirely natural, for the reason that a proper factor of n cannot exceed $\sqrt{n}$. So I started off in great excitement and confidence, and only after a week or so of agony came to realıze the true state of things. There was, however, a consolation prize. It occurred to me to try the reverse argument : I assumed R.H., operated (in the line of least resistance) with the integral function

$$\Pi\left\{\left(1+\frac{z}{p}\right)e^{-\frac{z}{p}}\right\}$$

and successfully deduced the P.N.T. This was just in time for my 1st Fellowship dissertation (September 1907); I suppressed it the following year.

I have a clear recollection of my youthful vıews about the P.N.T., and they illustrate the uncertainty of judgment and taste in a beginner in a field with no familiar land-marks. I was thrilled *myself* ; but didn't feel at all sure how the result would appeal to others, and if someone had said, ' not bad, but of course very special, not "proper" mathematics', I should have meekly acquiesced.   Hardy (a junior Fellowship Elector at the time) told me much later that he had ' courageously ' said at the time that it was the best thing in the dissertation, though without realizing it was submitted as original.   The dissertation as a whole was well received, and though I was passed over for a man at his last shot there was a gentleman's agreement that I should be elected next time.

From October 1907 to June 1910 I was Richardson lecturer at Manchester University.   At £250 this was better than the usual £150 or £120, and I was advised to take it, but it was a great mistake.   I could have stayed in Cambridge as a Research Scholar, and was soon offered the Allen Scholarship (incidentally tenable with a Fellowship if one got that later), but refused it to stay at Manchester.   I did not gain financially, but felt I needed a change from Cambridge.   If an austere desire for working at full stretch was also a motive it was fulfilled.   My work was as follows. 3 hours lecturing to a ' failed Matriculation ' class (the University earned fees by this) ;   3 hours to superior Intermediate ;   3 (possibly 2) hours to pupil teachers on ' Principles of Mathematics ' (an ' Education ' stunt, naturally a complete failure), 2 hours class-work with 3rd year Honours class, and 3 hours full-dress lectures to them. Most of the unoccupied time during the mornings was spent in a sort of ' class-work ' :   12 to 20 students sat doing examples, to be helped out when they got stuck ;   it is an admirable system (for the students).   Beyond this there was much paper work from the large elementary classes.   In any case, and whatever the details, what happened was 4 hours work of one sort or another on M., W., F. mornings, 3 hours Tu., Th. mornings ;   after lunch paper work and some lecture preparation done in a private room at the University and lasting from 2.30 to 4.0 or 4.30. (Elementary lectures we learned, of course, to deliver with a minimum of preparation, on occasion extempore.) Saturdays were free. But while for most of the staff the day's work ended by 4.30, I had high pressure work on top of the low pressure mountain. The 3rd year Honours class at that time got what was in spirit the most liberal mathematical education in the country. Unhampered by the official examinations, which were made to yield the results known to be right, we aimed at doing a few selected things really properly, dealt with some utilitarian stuff in class-work, and did not try to cover everything. The Pure side of this was my responsibility, and I had a completely free hand. One of my selections was Differential Geometry. This gave comparatively little trouble, since I stuck slavishly to my notes of Herman, except for a necessary dilution. (Many years later I mentioned this to Hardy, who confessed in return that when he found being Professor of Geometry at Oxford involved giving actual lectures in Geometry he did exactly the same thing.) For the rest my lectures were in analysis. These called for as much preparation as any I have given since, and I had to prepare them in the evenings. Hardy's *Pure Mathematics* and Bromwich's *Infinite Series* were not available the 1st year. I must have found Jordan no use for what I wanted ; Goursat's *Cours* I could have used to some extent, were it not for the almost incredible fact that I was unaware of its existence. It is hard to realize now the difficulty of planning a logical order that would not unexpectedly let one down (and my admiration for Bromwich's performance was unbounded). I aimed only at teaching a working efficiency (no elegance, but full rigour—and we dealt even in repeated infinite integrals), but it was exceedingly hard going. The lectures were fairly successful, and temporarily seduced Sydney Chapman into becoming an analyst. (I added to my difficulties by being one of the most feckless young men I know of ; my lecture notes were

F

not unnaturally scrawled, but they were on odd sheets and too chaotic to be used another year.) It remains to add to this story that the two long terms were 10-week, the only remission being that the Long Vacation began reasonably early in June. Work at this pressure (apart from my special difficulties) was the accepted thing, and research was supposed to be done in one's leisure : I remember one Easter vacation, when I was worn out and could not force myself to work, suffering pangs of conscience over my laziness. ' Young men of today don't know what work is.' I should add that H. Lamb (doubling the parts of Pure and Applied Professors) did his full share of the work, and showed me many kindnesses.

1 joined the Trinity staff in 1910 (succeeding Whitehead). This coincided with new mathematical interests. Landau's book on analytical number theory made exciting reading, and stimulated me to some ideas on the ζ-function, but I need not say anything about this. I have, however, some vivid, and to me amusing, recollections of the discovery of the proof of the ' Abel-Tauber Theorem ' (' if $\lim_{x \to 1} \Sigma a_n x^n = s$ and $a_n = O(1/n)$ then Σa_n converges to s '). This happened at Bideford in the Easter vacation of 1911. The problem had quite certainly been suggested by Hardy, but I was unaware that he had proved the (weaker) ' Cesàro-Tauber '. This is very strange. In the first place he had told me about it , but I suppose at a time when I had not begun to think actively in that field. On the other hand, I had at that time in high degree the flair of the young for tracking down any previous experience that might bear on the problem in hand ; this must have been out of action. But however strange, it was providential. The main theorem depends on 2 separate ideas, and one of them is the connexion between 3 (or more) successive derivates (if $f = o(1)$ and $f'' = O(1)$ then $f' = o(1)$ [1]). I began on the Cesàro-Tauber and in the course

---

[1] See p. 36, and footnote 1.

of finding a proof was led to the derivates theorem : but for this the derivates theorem would never have emerged out of the rut of the established proof (which differed a good deal), and without it 'I should never have got the main theorem. (The derivates theorem was actually known, but buried in a paper by Hadamard on waves.) It is of course good policy, and I have often practised it, to begin without going too much into the existing literature.

The derivates theorem enables one to reject certain parts of the thing one wants to tend to 0. One day I was playing round with this, and a ghost of an idea entered my mind of making r, the number of differentiations, *large*. At that moment the spring cleaning that was in progress reached the room I was working in, and there was nothing for it but to go walking for 2 hours, in pouring rain. The problem seethed violently in my mind : the material was disordered and cluttered up with irrelevant complications cleared away in the final version, and the ' idea ' was vague and elusive. Finally I stopped, in the rain, gazing blankly for minutes on end over a little bridge into a stream (near Kenwith wood), and presently a flooding certainty came into my mind that the thing was done. The 40 minutes before I got back and could verify were none the less tense.

On looking back this time seems to me to mark my arrival at a reasonably assured judgment and taste, the end of my ' education '. I soon began my 35-year collaboration with Hardy.

Review of Ramanujan's Collected Papers[1]

Collected Papers of Srinivasa Ramanujan. Edited by G. H. HARDY, P. V. SESHU AIGAR, and B. M. WILSON. Pp. xxxvi+355. 30s. net. 1927. (Cambridge Univ. Press.)

Ramanujan was born in India in December 1887, came to Trinity College, Cambridge, in April 1914, was ill from May 1917 onwards, returned to India in February 1919, and died in April 1920. He was a Fellow of Trinity and a Fellow of the Royal Society.

Ramanujan had no university education, and worked unaided in India until he was twenty-seven. When he was sixteen he came by chance on a copy of Carr's *Synopsis of Mathematics*; and this book, now sure of an immortality its author can hardly have dreamt of, woke him quite suddenly to full activity. A study of its contents is indispensable to any considered judgment. It gives a very full account of the purely formal side of the integral calculus, containing, for example, Parseval's formula, Fourier's repeated integral and other ' inversion formulae ', and a number of formulae of the type recognizable by the expert under the general description ' $f(a)=f(\beta)$ if $a\beta=\pi^2$ '. There is also a section on the transformation of power series into continued fractions. Ramanujan somehow acquired also an effectively complete knowledge of the formal side of the theory of elliptic functions (not in Carr). The matter is obscure, but this, together with what is to be found in, say, Chrystal's *Algebra*, seems to have been his complete equipment in analysis and theory of numbers. It is at least certain that he knew nothing of existing methods of working with divergent series, nothing of quadratic residuacity, nothing of work on the distribution of primes (he may have known Euler's formula $\Pi(1-p^{-s})^{-1}=\Sigma n^{-s}$, but not any

[1] Reprinted from the *Mathematical Gazette*, April 1929, Vol. XIV, No 200.

account of the ζ-function). Above all, he was totally ignorant of Cauchy's theorem and complex function-theory. (This may seem difficult to reconcile with his complete knowledge of elliptic functions. A sufficient, and I think a necessary, explanation would be that Greenhill's very odd and individual *Elliptic Functions* was his text-book.)

The work he published during his Indian period did not represent his best ideas, which he was probably unable to expound to the satisfaction of editors. At the beginning of 1914, however, a letter from Ramanujan to Mr. Hardy (then at Trinity, Cambridge) gave unmistakeable evidence of his powers, and he was brought to Trinity, where he had three years of health and activity. (Some characteristic work, however, belongs to his two years of illness)

I do not intend to discuss here in detail the work for which Ramanujan was solely responsible (a very interesting estimate is given by Prof. Hardy, p. xxxiv). If we leave out of account for the moment a famous paper written in collaboration with Hardy, his definite contributions to mathematics, substantial and original as they are, must, I think, take second place in general interest to the romance of his life and mathematical career, his unusual psychology, and above all to the fascinating problem of how great a mathematician he might have become in more fortunate circumstances. In saying this, of course, I am adopting the highest possible standard, but no other is appropriate.

Ramanujan's great gift is a 'formal' one; he dealt in 'formulae'. To be quite clear what is meant, I give two examples (the second is at random, the first is one of supreme beauty):

$$p(4) + p(9)x + p(14)x^2 + \cdots = 5\frac{\{(1-x^5)(1-x^{10})(1-x^{15}) \ldots\}^5}{\{(1-x)(1-x^2)(1-x^3) \ldots\}^6},$$

where $p(n)$ is the number of partitions of n;

$$\int_0^\infty \frac{\cos \pi x}{\{\Gamma(a+x)\Gamma(a-x)\}^2} \, dx = \frac{1}{4\Gamma(2a-1)\{\Gamma(a)\}^2} \quad (a > \tfrac{1}{2}).$$

But the great day of formulae seems to be over. No one, if we are again to take the highest standpoint, seems able to discover a radically new type, though Ramanujan comes near it in his work on partition series ; it is futile to multiply examples in the spheres of Cauchy's theorem and elliptic function theory, and some general theory dominates, if in a less degree, every other field. A hundred years or so ago his powers would have had ample scope. Discoveries alter the general mathematical atmosphere and have very remote effects, and we are not prone to attach great weight to re-discoveries, however independent they seem. How much are we to allow for this ; how great a mathematician might Ramanujan have been 100 or 150 years ago ; what would have happened if he had come into touch with Euler at the right moment ? How much does lack of education matter ? Was it formulae or nothing, or did he develop in the direction he did only because of Carr's book—after all, he learned later to do new things well, and at an age mature for an Indian ? Such are the questions Ramanujan raises ; and everyone has now the material to judge them. The letters and the lists of results announced without proof are the most valuable evidence available in the present volume ; they suggest, indeed, that the note-books would give an even more definite picture of the essential Ramanujan, and it is very much to be hoped that the editor's project of publishing them *in extenso* will eventually be carried out.

Carr's book quite plainly gave Ramanujan both a general direction and the germs of many of his most elaborate developments. But even with these partly derivative results one is impressed by his extraordinary profusion, variety, and power. There is hardly a field of formulae, except that of classical number-theory, that he has not enriched, and in which he has not revealed unsuspected possibilities. The beauty and singularity of his results is entirely uncanny. Are they odder than one would expect things selected for oddity to be ? The moral seems to be

that we never expect enough; the reader at any rate
experiences perpetual shocks of delighted surprise. And if
he will sit down to an unproved result taken at random, he
will find, if he can prove it at all, that there is at lowest some
' point ', some odd or unexpected twist. Prof. Watson and
Mr. Preece have begun the heroic task of working through
the unproved statements ; some of their solutions have
appeared recently in the *Journal of the London Mathematical
Society*, and these strongly encourage the opinion that a
complete analysis of the note-books will prove very well
worth while.

There can, however, be little doubt that the results showing
the most striking originality and the deepest insight are those
on the distribution of primes (see pp. xxii-xxv, xxvii, 351,
352). The problems here are not in origin formal at all ;
they concern approximate formulae for such things as the
number of primes, or of integers expressible as a sum of two
squares, less than a large number x ; and the determination
of the orders of the errors is a major part of the theory. The
subject has a subtle function-theory side ; it was inevitable
that Ramanujan should fail here, and that his methods
should lead him astray ; he predicts the approximate
formulae, but is quite wrong about the orders of the errors.
These problems tax the last resources of analysis, took over
a hundred years to solve, and were not solved at all before
1890 ; Ramanujan could not possibly have achieved
complete success. What he did was to perceive that an
attack on the problems could at least be begun on the
formal side, and to reach a point at which the main results
become plausible. The formulae do not in the least lie on
the surface, and his achievement, taken as a whole, is most
extraordinary.

If Carr's book gave him direction, it had at least nothing
to do with his *methods*, the most important of which were
completely original. His intuition worked in analogies,
sometimes remote, and to an astonishing extent by empirical

induction from particular numerical cases. Being without
Cauchy's theorem, he naturally dealt much in transforma-
tions and inversions of order of double integrals. But his
most important weapon seems to have been a highly
elaborate technique of transformation by means of divergent
series and integrals. ·(Though methods of this kind are of
course known, it seems certain that his discovery was quite
independent.) He had no strict logical justification for his
operations. He was not interested in rigour, which for that
matter is not of first-rate importance in analysis beyond the
undergraduate stage, and can be supplied, given a real idea,
by any competent professional. The clear-cut idea of what
is *meant* by a proof, nowadays so familiar as to be taken for
granted, he perhaps did not possess at all. If a significant
piece of reasoning occurred somewhere, and the total mixture
of evidence and intuition gave him certainty, he looked no
further. It is a minor indication of his quality that he can
never have *missed* Cauchy's theorem. With it he could have
arrived more rapidly and conveniently at certain of his
results, but his own methods enabled him to survey the
field with an equal comprehensiveness and as sure a grasp.

I must say something finally of the paper on partitions
(pp. 276-309) written jointly with Hardy. The number
$p(n)$ of the partitions of n increases rapidly with n, thus :

$$p(200) = 3972999029388.$$

The authors show that $p(n)$ is the integer nearest

(1) $$\frac{1}{2\sqrt{2}} \sum_{q=1}^{\nu} \sqrt{q} A_q(n) \psi_q(n),$$

where $A_q(n) = \sum \omega_{p,q} e^{-2np\pi i/q}$, the sum being over p's prime
to q and less than it, $\omega_{p,q}$ is a certain $24q$-th root of unity,
ν is of the order of $\sqrt{n}$, and

$$\psi_q(n) = \frac{d}{dn} (\exp\{C\sqrt{(n-\tfrac{1}{24})}/q\}), \quad C = \pi\sqrt{\tfrac{2}{3}}.$$

We may take $\nu=4$ when $n=100$. For $n=200$ we may take $\nu=5$; five terms of the series (1) predict the correct value of $p(200)$. We may always take $\nu=a\sqrt{n}$ (or rather its integral part), where a is any positive constant we please, provided n exceeds a value $n_0(a)$ depending only on a.

The reader does not need to be told that this is a very astonishing theorem, and he will readily believe that the methods by which it was established involve a new and important principle, which has been found very fruitful in other fields. The story of the theorem is a romantic one. (To do it justice I must infringe a little the rules about collaboration. I therefore add that Prof. Hardy confirms and permits my statements of bare fact.) One of Ramanujan's Indian conjectures was that the first term of (1) was a very good approximation to $p(n)$; this was established without great difficulty. At this stage the $n-\frac{1}{24}$ was represented by a plain n—the distinction is irrelevant. From this point the real attack begins. The next step in development, not a very great one, was to treat (1) as an ' asymptotic ' series, of which a fixed number of terms (e.g. $\nu=4$) were to be taken, the error being of the order of the next term. But from now to the very end Ramanujan always insisted that much more was true than had been established : ' there must be a formula with error $O(1)$ '. This was his most important contribution ; it was both absolutely essential and most extraordinary. A severe numerical test was now made, which elicited the astonishing facts about $p(100)$ and $p(200)$. Then ν was made a function of n ; this *was* a very great step, and involved new and deep function-theory methods that Ramanujan obviously could not have discovered by himself. The complete theorem thus emerged. But the solution of the final difficulty was probably impossible without one more contribution from Ramanujan, this time a perfectly characteristic one. As if its analytical difficulties were not enough, the theorem was entrenched also behind almost impregnable defences of a purely formal kind. The form of the function $\psi_q(n)$ is a kind of indivisible unit , among many asymptotically equivalent forms it is essential to select exactly the right one. Unless this is done at the outset, and the $-\frac{1}{24}$ (to say nothing of the d/dn) is an extraordinary stroke of formal genius, the complete result can never come into the picture at all. There is, indeed, a touch of real mystery. If only we *knew* there was a formula with error $O(1)$, we might be forced, by slow stages, to the correct form of ψ_q. But why was Ramanujan so certain there *was* one ? *Theoretical* insight, to be the explanation, had to be of an order hardly to be credited. Yet it is hard to see what numerical instances could have been available to suggest so strong a result. And unless the form of ψ_q was known already, *no* numerical evidence could suggest anything of the kind—there seems no escape, at least, from the conclusion that the discovery of the correct form was a single stroke of insight. We owe the theorem to a singularly happy collaboration of two men, of quite unlike gifts, in which each contributed the best, most characteristic, and most fortunate work that was in him   Ramanujan's genius did have this one opportunity worthy of it.

The volume contains a biography by the second of the editors, and the obituary notice by Prof. Hardy. These give quite a vivid picture of Ramanujan's interesting and attractive personality. The mathematical editors have done their work most admirably. It is very unobtrusive ; the reader is told what he wants to know at exactly the right moment, and more thought and bibliographical research must have gone into it than he is likely to suspect.

Three Reviews[1]

Cambridge Tracts on Mathematics and Mathematical Physics : No. 23. ' Operational Methods in Mathematical Physics.' By HAROLD JEFFREYS. No. 24. ' Invariants of Quadratical Differential Forms.' By OSWALD VEBLEN. (Cambridge University Press.) 6s. 6d. each.

The Theory of Functions of a Real Variable and the Theory of Fourier's Series. By E. W. HOBSON. Vol. 1, 3rd Edition. (Cambridge University Press.) 45s.

1. Every mathematical physicist should know Heaviside's operational methods, and Dr. Jeffrey's tract is welcome. The first three chapters deal with differential equations in one independent variable. This is a subject capable of rigour ; the purist, indeed, can cavil at nothing in the author's account except the omission of a consistency theorem on p. 25, line 4. In any specific problem the method has definite advantages over the ordinary one ; it avoids simultaneous equations for the arbitrary constants, is indifferent to multiple roots, and takes full advantage of any accidental simplicity.

If the method were confined to one variable it would hardly deserve a Cambridge tract. In Chapter IV, however, we come to two independent variables, and the reader enters a new and miraculous world (of which, indeed, he has already had startling glimpses on pp. 18, 22). A dozen pages later he meets arguments that do a good deal to diminish his misgivings, but in the last resort the method is not rigorously established ; it is best regarded as a heuristic process whose solutions require a final verification. Of its power and penetration in the discovery of solutions, however, there can be no doubt, and its practice is singularly agreeable.

Some of the applications use the so-called ' method of

---

[1] Reprinted from the *Cambridge Review*, May 4, 1928.

steepest descents '. The name embodies a rule for ascending a pass : ' keep to the stream '. But all ways up the valley are theoretically equivalent, and the stream is not invariably the most convenient one ; the non-commital ' saddle-point method ' is a preferable name. In the exposition there is a familiar difficulty ; the simplest case of all is clear, but each of several elaborations has its own set of troubles.   A judicious vagueness enables the author to hit off, as usual, a satisfactory compromise. His treatment is a little careless in detail, and surely never has the square root of a harmless complex number been so horridly dismembered (pp. 78, 79).

The reader who embarks upon the considerable and growing literature referred to in the bibliography will begin to realize the admirable judgment with which Dr. Jeffreys has steered between difficulties, and his skill in keeping his account simple. To some minds the theory will be most interesting where it is wildest. It gives correct results in far wider fields than are covered by any of the rigorous interpretations ; does this mean that there must be a point of view in which all is plain and demonstrable ? Such a belief seems the right interpretation of the tract's concluding passage, which must otherwise be attributed to pure mysticism. The reviewer is sceptical, but the possibility is alluring.

2. For the latest Cambridge tract the editors have been able to secure an author who is one of the most eminent of living mathematicians, a distinguished contributor to the subject on which he writes, and a master of exposition. Professor Veblen's first four chapters (half the book) develop the analytical theory of differential invariants without any sidelight from physics or geometry. Thus it comes about that while Parts I and II of Levi-Civita's ' The absolute differential calculus '—equally pure mathematics—is easy reading, this part of the book is decidedly stiff. This, however, is through no fault of the author. It is simply that an affine connexion, considered abstractly, is very far from being a joke. As a first approach to Relativity these

chapters are probably impenetrable. The amateur relativist with some previous knowledge should be able to master it at, say, his second reading ; in his first, if he is a pure mathematician, his contented purr at a definition of invariance that really means something may become in the end a sigh for the more easy-going ways of the physicists. The reader will be wise also not to start with a preconceived idea of the number of pages he reads in an hour : the author's style is of the kind that uses no unnecessary word, and the argument is extremely concentrated.

Chapter IV illustrates the general theory by its simplest case, Euclidean geometry. Chapter V discusses the equivalence problem (the simplest case of which is applicability of surfaces) and includes some very general theorems. The tract ends with a chapter on normal co-ordinates.

The book should be read by every relativist ; the first part on the ground that the subject should be studied in every fundamental aspect ; the second if only for the account of normal co-ordinates, an important subject that is very little known.

3. After the prodigious labours of his Vol. II, Professor Hobson must have found his third edition of Vol. I almost child's play. There are a fair number of minor changes, of which it is perhaps enough to mention the rewriting and expansion of the section on the Riemann-Stieltjes integral, a conception whose field of application steadily widens.

Is it necessary for analysts to lie down under the wellworn gibe about ' pathology of functions ', even as little as Professor Hobson does ? If there was once a fashion for destroying plausible conjectures by the invention of suitably misbehaving functions, it came to an end at least twenty years ago. The very great majority of theorems proved since then are assertions of positive and elegant behaviour : ' pathological ' theorems are sometimes needed to round off the positive ones, but they are essentially secondary and with rare exceptions easy.

Newton and the Attraction of a Sphere[1]

1. In Keynes's contribution to the ' Newton Tercentenary Celebrations ' there is the following passage :

' Again, there is some evidence that Newton in preparing the *Principia* was held up almost to the last moment by lack of proof that you could treat a solid sphere as though all its mass were concentrated at the centre, and only hit on the proof a year before publication. But this was a truth which he had known for certain and had always assumed for many years.

' Certainly there can be no doubt that the peculiar geometrical form in which the exposition of the *Principia* is dressed up bears no resemblance at all to the mental processes by which Newton actually arrived at his conclusions.

' His experiments were always, I suspect, a means, not of discovery, but always of verifying what he knew already.'

To know things by intuition happens to humbler people, and it happened, of course, to Newton in supreme degree; but I should be inclined to doubt this particular example, even in the absence of evidence. Many things are not accessible to intuition at all, the value of $\int_0^\infty e^{-x^2} dx$ for instance. The ' central ' attraction of a sphere is, of course, more arguable, but in point of fact Newton says in his letter to Halley of 20th June, 1686, that until 1685 [probably early spring] he suspected it to be false. (For the letter, see Rouse Ball, *An Essay on Newton's Principia*, pp. 156-159 ; the critical passage is from 1. 7 on, p. 157.

[1] Reprinted from the *Mathematical Gazette*, July 1948, Vol. XXXII, No. 300.

See also p. 61.) There is, I think, a sufficient and fairly plausible explanation for the proof being held up, and an analysis of the mathematical setting of the problem is of interest.

2. I take it as established that Newton did not believe in the central attraction before 1685. This being so he may well have thought the determination of the actual attraction a detail to be considered later. (It is true that in the 1666 comparison of the attraction at the moon's distance with that at the surface of the earth the departure from centrality at the surface, being at its worst, would be a serious matter. This, however, merely adds further mystery to a subject already sufficiently obscure. It is odd, incidentally, that all the accounts of the matter that I have come across before 1947 ignore this particular point.) He did, however, attack the problem in the end. Now, *with a knowledge of the answer*, the problem reduces at once to the attraction of a spherical *shell*, which in straightforward integration in cartesians happens to reduce to integration of the function $(ax+b)/(cx+d)^2$, child's play to Newton. *Without* this knowledge it is natural to attack the solid sphere , this is more formidable, and may have baffled him until he had fully developed his calculus methods. To the Newton of 1685 the problem was bound to yield in reasonable time : it is possible (though this is quite conjectural) that he tried the approach *via* a shell of radius r, to be followed by an integration with respect to r ; this would of course instantly succeed. Anyhow he found a proof (and after that would always deal with the shell). But this was by no means the end of the matter. What he had to find was, as we all know, a proof, no doubt a calculus one in the first instance, which would ' translate ' into geometrical language. Let the reader try.

I think we can infer with some plausibility what the calculus proof was, and I give it in modern dress. It operates, of course, on the *shell*.

* 3. The figure is Newton's except that I have added the dotted line SH and marked three angles.

Let $SH=a$, $SP=r$. The variable of integration is taken

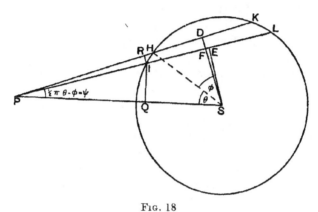

FIG. 18

to be ϕ.[1] Consider the zone generated by rotation of HI round SP, and its (resolved) contribution $\delta F = \delta F_P$ to the total attraction F_P on P. This contribution satisfies

$$r^2 \frac{\delta F}{\delta \phi} = \left(\frac{PS}{PI}\right)^2 \cos\psi \cdot 2\pi a \mid \delta\theta \mid IQ \cdot \frac{1}{\delta\phi},$$

(1) $$\frac{r^2 \, dF}{a^2 \, d\phi} = \left(\frac{\cos\phi}{\sin\theta}\right)^2 \sin(\theta+\phi) \sin\theta \left|\frac{d\theta}{d\phi}\right|.$$

From triangle PHS we have

$$\frac{\cos(\theta+\phi)}{\cos\phi} = \frac{a}{r},$$

whence

(2) $$\frac{d\theta}{d\phi} = 1 - \tan\phi \, \cot(\theta+\phi) = -\frac{\sin\theta}{\sin(\theta+\phi)\cos\phi}.$$

---

[1] The order of lettering significantly corresponds to a *positive* increment $\delta\phi$.

From (1) and (2),

$$(3) \qquad \frac{r^2}{2\pi a^2}\frac{dF}{d\phi}=\cos\phi.$$

The range R of ϕ is $-\tfrac12\pi$ to $\tfrac12\pi$, and we should arrive at the appropriate result by integration. Newton's argument, however, is in effect that R is independent of P, so that for two positions P, p, we have [1] $F_p/F_p=Sp^2/SP^2$.

4. Now for the geometrical proof (which must have left its readers in helpless wonder) There is a counterpart figure in small letters (the two spheres being equal). The use of ϕ-integration translates into the 'peculiar' idea 'let phk cut off an arc hk equal to HK, and similarly for pil'. The details that follow are in essentials elegant and very carefully arranged, but the archaic language makes for heavy going, and I modernise. The *difficulties* arise from (2), naturally troublesome to translate.

Since $hk=HK$ and $il=IL$, we have

$$(4) \qquad se=SE, \quad df(=sd-se=SD-SE)=DF.$$

The contributions $\delta F_{P,p}$ of the two respective incremental zones of HI, hi satisfy

$$(5) \qquad \frac{\delta F_p}{\delta F_P}=\frac{PI^2}{pi^2}\cdot\left(\frac{pf}{ps}\Big/\frac{PF}{PS}\right)\cdot\frac{hi\cdot iq}{HI\cdot IQ}.$$

Also

$$\frac{pf\cdot PI}{pi\cdot PF}=\frac{pf}{pi}\Big/\frac{PF}{PI}=\frac{df}{ri}\Big/\frac{DF}{RI}=\frac{RI}{ri}$$

$$(6) \qquad =\frac{IH}{ih},$$

since $\angle RHI=\angle rhi$. From $PI/PS=IQ/SE$, its counterpart, and $SE=se$, we have

$$(7) \qquad \frac{PI}{PS}\Big/\frac{pi}{ps}=\frac{IQ}{iq}.$$

[1] This is the statement of the crucial 'Prop. 71'. The constant is actually never determined

G

Multiplying (6) and (7) we have

$$\frac{PI^2 \cdot pf \cdot ps}{pi^2 \cdot PF \cdot PS} = \frac{IH \cdot IQ}{ih \cdot iq} ,$$

which combines with (5) to give

$$\frac{\delta F_p}{\delta F_P} = \frac{PS^2}{ps^2} .$$

5. There is a proof satisfying Newton's canons, which one feels he might have arrived at if he had found no other way. It arises easily enough out of the modern approach and is as follows : it operates on the solid sphere. (The original notation P, S is being continued.)

Consider Σ, the concentric sphere through P, the component attraction $N_Q(P)$ at P normal to Σ of a unit particle at Q, and the average $\bar{N}_Q$ of $N_Q(P)$ over all P of Σ. The contribution to the total $4\pi a^2 \bar{N}_Q$, i.e. average multiplied by area, of an element of area $\delta\Sigma$ is, by easy geometry, the solid angle subtended by $\delta\Sigma$ at Q. Hence $4\pi a^2 \bar{N}_Q = 4\pi$, and $\bar{N}_Q$ is independent of Q and so equal to $\bar{N}_S$. Now $\Sigma\bar{N}_Q \delta V_Q$, taken over elements of volume of the solid sphere, is the average normal attraction of the solid sphere taken over points of Σ, and its equivalent $\bar{N}_S \Sigma \delta V_Q$ is the corresponding thing for the mass concentrated at S. In each case the thing averaged is constant and equal to the *total* force, and the equivalence gives what we want.

6. Return to the question of ' intuition '. The obvious argument ' against ' is : ' What has the inverse square got that the inverse cube hasn't ? ' There is an answer to this : the inverse square is the ' natural ' law of diminution with distance, e.g. of light or sound, and others than Newton thought of it in connexion with the planetary system.[1]

---

[1] It may be observed that with a law r^{-0} the attraction at the surface of the solid sphere is less than the central value, while with a law r^{-4} it is greater. These facts are obvious, in the second case because the attraction concerned is infinite.

Alternatively, adopt a corpuscular theory of light, in which corpuscles from different origins do not collide. If they are, say, inelastic, the corpuscles from a point create a *repulsion* according to the inverse square, and *the total pressure on a sphere with the point as centre is independent of the radius*. This independence, combined with the symmetry, might produce the feeling that the situation in the original attraction problem is best compatible with 'centrality': an intuition. But by this time we are within striking distance of the proof given above. The total outward (i.e. normal) pressure on a Σ due to an origin of corpuscles at Q is a not unnatural idea, and the key is to prove that it is independent of the position of Q.★

Large Numbers [1]

§ 1. The problem how to express very large numbers is discussed in ' The Sand-Reckoner ' of Archimedes. Grains of sand being proverbially ' innumerable ', Archimedes develops a scheme, the equivalent of a 10^n notation, in which the ' Universe ', a sphere reaching to the sun and calculated to have a diameter less than 10^{10} stadia, would contain, if filled with sand, fewer grains than ' 1000 units of the seventh order of numbers ', which is 10^{51}. [A myriad-myriad is 10^8 , this is taken as the base of what we should call exponents, and Archimedes contemplates 10^8 ' periods ', each containing 10^8 ' orders ' of numbers ; the final number in the scheme is $10^{8 \cdot 10^{15}}$.] The problem of expression is bound up with the invention of a suitable *notation* ; Archimedes does not have our a^b, with its potential extension to a^{a^a} . We return to this question at the end ; the subject is not exhausted.

§ 2. Certain ancient Indian writings reveal an awestruck obsession with ideas of immense stretches of time. See Buckle's *History of Civilisation in England,* pp. 121-124 (2nd edition). (I *thought* the following came from there ; I cannot have invented it, surely.)

There is a stone, a cubic mile in size, a million times harder than diamond. Every million years a very holy man visits it to give it the lightest possible touch. The stone is in the end worn away. This works out at something like 10^{35} years ; poor value for so much trouble, and an instance of the ' debunking ' of popular immensities.

[1] Reprinted from the *Mathematical Gazette*, July 1948, Vol. XXXII, No. 300   Additions in square brackets.

§ 3. The Greeks made an enormous leap of the imagination in conceiving the heavenly bodies as objects dispersed in ' ordinary ' space. A similar if lesser leap was needed to initiate the now familiar geological arguments about erosion and the like. It is easy to imagine Archimedes doing this, but so far as I know no Greek did. It can be a mildly entertaining exercise to check, for example, the scooping out of a valley by a trickle of stream, unthinkable to common sense. A twentieth of an inch a year is a mile in 10^6 years; this, if continued, would be a thousand miles in 10^9 years. (These times are natural units; the second is comparable with the age of the earth, the first is the time it takes to turn an ape into a Ph.D.)

Newton estimated the distance of Sirius (in astronomical units), assuming it to be comparable with the sun. His method was to compare Sirius and Saturn, guessing (correctly) the albedo of the latter.

§ 4. The next two items complete my references to the past. The first is the accuracy of Tycho Brahe's angular measurements. These were correct to 1′, which I find surprising (Hipparchus's to 4′). The other is the Samos tunnel, described in Farrington's very interesting Pelican book, *Greek Science*, p. 37. Made at about the time of Pythagoras, it was 900 yards long and was begun at opposite ends; the junction in the middle is shown by modern digging to have been within a couple of feet. I am not concerned with the mild ideological axe-grinding of the book, but it is surely simplest to disbelieve that this was an achievement of surveying technique. The relevant *principles* of similar triangles existed since Thales, but I find the instrumental accuracy incredible. I can, on the other hand, easily believe in a line of posts over the hill, or at a pinch in sighting on a star from opposite sides.

§ 5.   I come to modern times, but continue the topic of measurements.

We all know that measured parallaxes deal in quantities of the order of $0''\cdot001$ (average error $0''\cdot025$) ; does every reader realize that this is the angle subtended by a penny 4000 miles away ?

Astronomical measurement of time provides the greatest number of significant figures used in scientific calculation ; measurement is to $\cdot001''$, it is possible to deal in 10^2 or 10^3 years, and with a couple of extra figures for purposes of calculation we have a total of 15.

I once asked Eddington what accuracy was possible in measuring the angular separation of widely separated stars. To the outsider the mechanical difficulties seem enormous, as do those of dealing with refraction ; the answer (given instantly) was $0''\cdot1$, which I for one found very surprising.

I will hand on another surprise.   The principles of an Ordnance Survey clearly involve, first, something of the nature of a ' rod ', which is placed in successive positions until we arrive, secondly, at a ' base ', from which we carry on by angular measurements.   The questions are : what are the most efficient lengths of rod and base ?   The ' rod ' is a metal ribbon 130 inches long, which is much what anyone would expect ; but the length of the base, which is 9 miles, is about 100 times what I should have guessed.   In such matters, of course, the really determining difficulty is apt to be something not obvious and interesting, but unexpected and dull : apparently the trouble is that of placing a theodolite accurately over the right spot.

§ 6.   We shall presently be considering multiple exponentials and we must consider the principles of their ' approximate ' nature.   Since ' order ' has a technical meaning not suited to our purposes, we will speak of ' types ' of numbers,

$$N_1 = 10^{10}, \quad N_2 = 10^{10^{10}}, \ \ldots, \quad N_n = 10^{N_{n-1}},$$

which we describe as of type 1, 2, ... , n, ... We further

describe $$10^{10^{10^{4\cdot7}}},$$

for example, as of type 2·47, and write it $N_{2\cdot47}$. This makes the point that its type is between 2 and 3 ; there is a slight inaccuracy in that it is $N_{2\cdot1}$ and not $N_{2\cdot0}$ that is N_2—we may ignore this. We also call it $N_2(4\cdot7)$ when we wish to express its mathematical form in brief notation : note that N_n is $N_n(1)$. The number 10^{79}, which (with apologies for the small letter) we will call u, as being the number of ultimate particles in the Universe, is $N_{1\cdot19}$.

The principle I now wish to establish is sufficiently illustrated by the following instances. A number of type 2 or over is ' practically unaltered ' by being squared , a number of type 3 or over is what we may fairly call ' unaltered ' by being raised even to the power u. In fact, while

$$N_2 = 10^{10^{10}},$$

we have $\qquad N_2{}^2 = 10^{10^{10\cdot3}};$

and while $\qquad N_3 = N_3(1),$

we have $\qquad N_3{}^u = N_3(1 + 7\cdot9 \,.\, 10^{-9}).$

Again, N_2 is hardly altered by having its bottom 10 changed into u, and is ' unaltered ' by having it changed into 2. Another constantly relevant point is that for an N of type 1 or over there is ' no difference ' between N ! (or N^N) and 2^N.

We may sum up these considerations as the ' principle of crudity ' : the practical upshot is that in estimating a number a^{b^c} it is worth taking trouble to whittle down the top index, but we can be as crude as we like about things that bear only on the lowest ones.

§ 7. I come now to numbers directly connected with daily life (what I mean by ' indirectly ' will appear in § 11).

The range from just perceptible to just tolerable sound (at the same pitch, and where sensitivity is maximal) is over 10^{12}. In the case of light the range is (as we should expect) even greater. The surface of the sun has $6 . 10^5$ times the brightness of the full moon (incidentally the sun is $5 . 10^6$ times as bright as the *half* moon). A sandy surface lit by the full moon is accordingly in a similar relation with the surface of the full moon. Anyone who has walked on a country road on a moonless night with heavy cloud knows that one can still perceive the road or objects on it (I am not myself satisfied that anyone has properly explained where the light comes from) ; there must be a new factor of at least 10^3 (I should say 10^4 or more), the total being 10^{14} or 10^{15}.

At one time it was possible to buy 10^{13} ergs for 4d. ; nothing about energy of mass, merely the British Heat Unit : the erg is, of course, absurdly small, and the mechanical equivalent of heat very large.

Coincidences and Improbabilities

§ 8. Improbabilities are apt to be overestimated. It is true that I should have been surprised in the past to learn that Professor Hardy had joined the Oxford Group. But one could not say the adverse chance was $10^6 : 1$. Mathematics is a dangerous profession ; an appreciable proportion of us go mad, and then this particular event would be quite likely.

A popular newspaper noted during the 1947 cricket season that two batsmen had each scored 1111 runs for an average of 44·44. Since it compared this with the monkeys' typing of *Hamlet* (somewhat to the disadvantage of the latter) the event is worth debunking as an example of a common class (the same paper later gave a number of similar cases). We have, of course, to estimate the probability of the event happening at some time during the season. Take the 30 leading batsmen and select a pair A, B of them. At some moment A will have played 25 complete innings. The chance against his score then being 1111 is say 700 : 1. The chance against B's having at that moment played 25 innings is say 10 : 1, and the further chance that his score is 1111 is again 700 · 1. There are, however, about 30 . 15 pairs [1] ; the total adverse chance is 10 . $700^2/(30 . 15)$, or about 10^4 : 1. A modest degree of surprise is legitimate.

A report of holding 13 of a suit at Bridge used to be an annual event. The chance of this in a given deal is 2·4 . 10^{-9} ; if we suppose that 2 . 10^6 people in England each play an average of 30 hands a week the probability is of the right order. I confess that I used to suppose that Bridge hands were not random, on account of inadequate shuffling ; Borel's book on Bridge, however, shows that since the distribution within the separate hands is irrelevant the usual procedure of shuffling is adequate. (There is a marked difference where games of Patience are concerned : to destroy all organisation far more shuffling is necessary than one would naturally suppose ; I learned this from experience during a period of addiction, and have since compared notes with others.)

I sometimes ask the question what is the most remarkable coincidence you have experienced, and is it, for *the* most remarkable one, remarkable ? (With a lifetime to choose from, 10^6 : 1 is a mere trifle.) This is, of course, a subject made for bores, but I own two, one startling at the moment but debunkable, the other genuinely remarkable. In the latter a girl was walking along Walton St. (London) to visit her sister, Florence Rose Dalton, in service at number 42. She passed number 40 and arrived at 42, where a Florence Rose Dalton was cook (but absent for a fortnight's holiday, deputised for by her sister). But the house was 42 Ovington Sq. (the exit of the Square narrows to road width), 42 Walton St. being the house next further on. (I

---

[1] Note that it is pairs and not ordered pairs that are relevant.

was staying at the Ovington Sq. house and heard of the occurrence the same evening.)   In the other, 7 ships in Weymouth Harbour at the beginning of a 3 mile walk had become 6 when we sat down to rest :   the 6 were riding parallel at their anchors, but the two-masted 7th had aligned itself exactly behind a mast of one of the 6.   A shift of 5 yards clearly separated the masts.   The chance against stopping in the right 10 yards is $600 : 1$, that against the ship being end on about $60 . 1$; in all about $4.10^4 . 1$; the event is thus comparable to the cricket average both in striking impact and real insignificance.

There must exist a collection of well-authenticated co-incidences, and I regret that I am not better acquainted with them.   Dorothy Sayers in *Unpopular Opinions*, cites the case of two negroes, each named Will West, confined simultaneously in Leavenworth Penitentiary, U.S.A. (in 1903), and with the same Bertillon measurements.   (Is this really credible ?)

Eddington once told me that information about a new (newly visible, not necessarily unknown) comet was received by an Observatory in misprinted form ; they looked at the place indicated (no doubt sweeping a square degree or so), and saw a new comet.   (Entertaining and striking as this is the adverse chance can hardly be put at more than a few times 10^6.)

§ 9.   We all remember the schoolboy doodle of tracing a pencil line down a printed page through the spaces between words.   Suppose we take a small-print encyclopedia with about 100 lines to the page, and slash a line through at random.   With a $5 : 1$ chance against succeeding at a given line the chance against performing this doodle is 10^{70}.

My next instance is perhaps off the main track.   There is a certain procedure by which a conjuror may perform the apparently impossible.   A card, say the Ace of Spades, being selected the conjuror places the pack on the table and asks the subject to think of a number less than 100. There is a very fair chance that he will select 37 ; in this case he is told to count down and take the 37th card (which is the Ace) : if another number is selected *the conjuror does some other trick.* (A milder form deals with numbers less than 10 , the selection is very likely to be 7, and if not, then 3 , with 9 cards, and the Ace 7th he succeeds outright in the first case and can proffer the inverted pack in the second.)

In my present category belongs the chance typing of *Hamlet* by the monkeys. With say 27,000 letters and spaces to be typed and say 35 keys the adverse chance is $35^{27000} < N_{1\,5}$.

Games

§ 10. Suppose that in a game of position there are p possible positions $P_1, P_2, \ldots, P_p$. A game is a finite sequence of P's, each derived from the preceding by a ' move ' in accordance with the rules. p is generally of type slightly greater than 1, and the number of games may consequently be comparable with $p!$ or 2^p, which brings us for the first time to a type above 2. The crudity principle will be in operation.

In Chess, a game is a draw if the same position occurs for the 3rd time in all. (As a matter of fact the game continues unless one of the players exercises the right to claim a draw ; to avoid the consequent infinity we will suppose there *is* a draw.) The rules do not say whether for this purpose the men (' man '=' piece or pawn ') retain their identity ; we shall suppose that they do.[1]

What is the chance that a person A, ignorant of the rules will defeat C, the world champion ? Suppose that in practice C, in 1 out of n of his games, loses in not more than

---

[1] I learn from Mr H A Webb that in one of Blackburne's games a position recurred for a second time, but with a pair of rooks interchanged. Each player expected to win, otherwise (as Blackburne said) a delicate point for decision would have arisen.

m moves. We suppose that A knows that when it is his turn to move he must place one of his men on an unoccupied square, or on an enemy-occupied square, with capture. When he has $N \leqslant 16$ men he has a choice of $N^{64-N} \leqslant M = 16^{48}$ actions. There is, in effect, once in n games, a sequence of m actions leading to victory; his chance in all is better than $1 : nM^m$. The number n hardly matters if we can reduce m; if we may suppose [1] that m is 20 for $n = 10^6$, A has a chance better than $10^{-122} = 1/N_{1\,21}$ (more likely than two in succession of the doodles of § 9).

What is the number of possible games of Chess? It is easy to give an upper bound. A placing (legal or not) of men on the squares of the board we will call an ' arrangement ', A, one possible in Chess we will call a ' position ', P. A change from one A to another we call a 'shift ', and a legal Chess move (from a P) a ' move '. With N men in all on the board there are (with the ' individuality ' convention) $64!/(64-N)!$ A's. (As a matter of fact, since *all* pawns can be promoted, it is possible for something like this number to be actually P's when $N \leqslant 48$; the main legal bars are that the K's must not be contiguous, nor both in check, and that if there are 10 white (or black) bishops, they cannot all be on squares of one colour). The number of sets of men (irrespective of their placing) composed of pawns and pawns promoted (to Q, R, B or Kt) is
$$5^{16} + 5^{15} + \ldots + 5^1 < 2 \cdot 10^{11}.$$

Since the two K's must be present the number of sets of *pieces* other than those promoted from pawns is
$$_{14}C_1 + _{14}C_2 + \ldots + _{14}C_{14} < 14 \cdot _{14}C_7 < 5 \cdot 10^4;$$
hence the number of sets of N men is for every N less than 10^{16}.

The number of moves possible from a P (or for that matter an A) is at most
$$\mu = 9 \cdot 28 + 2 \cdot 14 + 2 \cdot 14 + 2 \cdot 8 + 8 = 332.$$

---

[1] We may suppose that C (in the light of A's performance !) does not suspect the position, and resigns in the ordinary way.

The number of A is less than

$$a = 10^{16} \sum_{N=1}^{32} \frac{64!}{(64-N)!} = 10^{69\ 7}.$$

The number of possible games is at most

$$\mu^{2a+1} = 10^{10^{70\ 5}} = N_{2\ 185}.$$

The problem of a not too hopelessly inadequate lower bound (even a moral certainty without full proof) seems not at all easy. Unless there are a fair number of mobile men the number of positions, which dominates the top index, is inadequate ; with a number of men, however, it is difficult to secure their *independent* ranging through long sequences of moves. We may consider Kings at corners protected from check by 3 minor pieces, and some Queens of each colour (9 if possible). I have thought of this question too late to try to develop a technique ; perhaps some readers may compete for a record.

§ 11. We come now to the numbers that I describe as indirectly connected with daily life. These arise out of the enormous number $n_0 = 3 . 10^{19}$ of molecules per c.c. of gas under standard conditions, and the permutations connected with them. I will recall the admirable illustration of Jeans that each time one of us draws a breath it is highly probable that it contains some of the molecules of the dying breath of Julius Caesar.

What is the probability that the *manuscript* (as opposed to a typescript) of *Hamlet* came into existence by chance ; say the probability that each of the n molecules of the ink found its chance way from an ink-pot into *some* point of an ink-line of script recognisable as the text of *Hamlet* ? We can choose half the molecules in the actual ink-line to determine a narrow region into which the other $\frac{1}{2}n$ molecules have to find their chance way. If the chance for a single molecule is f the relevant chance is $f^{\frac{1}{2}n}$. Since n is of the order of $500n_0 = 1 \cdot 5 \, . \, 10^{21}$, the crudity principle operates, and it makes no difference whether f is 10^{-1} or 10^{-10}. The adverse chance is $N_{2 \cdot 13}$.

We believe, of course, that something happened which at first sight is much more improbable ; the ink came into position in orderly succession in time. But what is the additional factor ? If we call the ink of a full stop a ' spot ', the ink-line is made up of say $s = 10^6$ spots. We must multiply the original number by $s!$, but this leaves it quite unaffected. (Similarly the latitude of choice implied by the italicised ' *some* ' above makes no difference.)

§ 12. We all know that it is merely probable, not certain, that a kettle on a gas-ring will boil. Let us estimate the chance, by common consent small, that a celluloid mouse should survive for a week in Hell (or alternatively that a real mouse should freeze to death). Piety dictates that we should treat the problem as classical, and suppose that the molecules and densities are terrestrial. We must not belittle the Institution, and will suppose a temperature (absolute) of $T_H = 2 \cdot 8 \, . \, 10^{12}$ (the $2 \cdot 8$ is put in to simplify my arithmetic).
* Let c be the velocity appropriate to temperature T, $T_0 = 280$ (English room temperature), $c_0 = c(T_0)$, $c_H = c(T_H)$. Let $\mu = kn_0$ be the number of molecules in the mouse ($k = 10^3$, say). The chance p that a given molecule has $c \leqslant c_0$ is, in the usual notation,

$$4\pi \int_0^{c_0} \left(\frac{hm}{\pi} \right)^{3/2} e^{-hmc^2} c^2 dc.$$

This is of order (the constant is irrelevant by the crudity principle)
$$p = (c_0/c_H)^3 = (T_0/T_H)^{3/2}.$$

The chance that most of the mouse has $c \leqslant c_0$ is not much better than p^μ. Let τ be the ' time of relaxation ' at temperature T ; this is comparable with the time of describing a free path ; then

$$\tau_H = \tau_0 c_0/c_H = \tau_0 (T_0/T_H)^{1/2},$$

and τ_0 is of order $\qquad \tau_0 = n_0^{-1/3}/c_0.$

In a week there are $\nu = w/\tau_H$ time intervals of length τ_H, where w is the number of seconds in a week.

Now an abnormal state subsides in time of order τ_H, and a fresh 'miracle' is needed for survival over the next interval. The total adverse chance against survival for a week is therefore of type

$$C = (p^{-\mu})' \cdot \left(\sqrt{\frac{T_H}{T_0}} \right)^{\frac{3}{2} c_0 \, ktc \, n_0^{4/3} \sqrt{\frac{T_H}{T_0}}} \star$$

With numerical values

$$n_0 = 3 \cdot 10^{19}, \; k = 10^3, \; c_0 = 4 \cdot 10^5, \; w = 5 \cdot 10^5, \; \sqrt{(T_H/T_0)} = 10^5,$$

we have $\qquad C = 10^{10^{46 \cdot 1}} = N_{2 \cdot 17}.$

Of the 46·1, 5 comes from T_H/T_0, 5·7 from w, 5·6 from c_0, and most from n_0.

Factorizations

§ 13. The days are past when it was a surprise that a number could be proved prime, or again composite, by processes other than testing for factors up to the square root ; most readers will have heard of Lehmer's electric sieve, and some at least will know of his developments of the 'converse of Fermat's theorem' by which the tests have been much advanced.[1] For comparison with our other numbers I will merely recall : $2^{127} - 1 \sim 10^{38}$ is the greatest known prime , $2^{257} - 1 \sim 10^{76}$ is composite though no factor is known, and it holds the record in that field ; $2^{2^6} + 1 \sim 10^{19}$ has factors $\qquad 274177 \quad$ and $\quad 67280421310721.$

[1] See *Math Ann.* 109 (1934), 661-667 ; *Bull. Amer. Math. Soc* 1928, 54-56 , *Amer. Math. Monthly*, 43 (1936), 347-354.

Most numbers that have been studied have naturally been of special forms like $a^n \pm b^n$; these are amenable to special tests of ' converse Fermat ' type. I asked Professor Lehmer what size of number N, taken at random, could be factorized, or again have its prime or composite nature determined, within, say, a year, and (a) for certain, (b) with reasonable certainty, (c) with luck. Much depends on the nature of $N-1$. If a reasonably large factor or product of factors of this is known the ' converse Fermat ' processes will decide the nature of N, and this for N with 50 to 100 digits. Similar results can be obtained if we can find factors of $N+1$. Generally both $N \pm 1$ will have many small factors. The disaster of finding all three of N, $N-1$, $N+1$ resisting factorization must be exceedingly rare (and it suggests theoretical investigation). If, however, it occurs the value of $a^N - 1 \pmod{N}$, with, say, $a=2$, can be calculated. If this is different from 1 then N is, of course, composite, if N *is* composite, the test, if we may judge by smaller N (of order 10^{10}), is very likely though not certain to succeed. If the value is 1, N is (accordingly) very likely but not certain to be prime. In this final case there remains, for definite proof, none but ' direct ' methods, and these are applicable only up to about 10^{20}.

Professor Lehmer further tells me that numbers up to $2 \cdot 7 \cdot 10^9$ can be completely factorized in 40 minutes ; up to 10^{15} in a day ; up to 10^{20} in a week ; finally up to 10^{100}, with some luck, in a year.

[Electronic calculating machines have now entered the field. The record prime is now $180p^2 + 1$, where p is the previous record prime $2^{127} - 1$. After 7 abortive tests on other numbers of the form $kp^2 + 1$ this successful one was recently made by J. C. P. Miller and D. J. Wheeler with the EDSAC at Cambridge. A converse Fermat test was used and the time occupied was 27 minutes.

The stop-press news (December 1952) is that Lehmer has found a prime greater than 2^{1000}.]

★ $\pi(x)-\mathrm{li}(x)$ *and the Skewes number*

§ 14.   The difference $d(x)=\pi(x)-\mathrm{li}\,x$, where $\pi(x)$ is the number of primes less than or equal to x, and li x is the (principal value) logarithmic integral $\int_{0}^{x}\dfrac{dx}{\log x}$, is negative for all x up to 10^7 and for all x for which $\pi(x)$ has been calculated.   I proved in 1914 that there must exist an X such that $d(x)$ is positive for some $x\leqslant X$.   It appeared later that this proof is a pure existence theorem and does not lead to any explicit numerical value of X ;   such a numerical value, free of hypotheses, was found by Dr. Skewes in 1937 ; his work has not yet been published, though it should be before very long.   In the meantime I will report here on the matter, for there are unexpected features apart from the size of the final X.

If we denote by θ the upper bound of the real parts of the complex zeros of the Riemann ζ-function $\zeta(s)$, the famous ' Riemann hypothesis ' (R.H. for short) is that $\theta=\tfrac{1}{2}$;   if this is false, then $\tfrac{1}{2}<\theta\leqslant1$.   It has long been known that in the latter case $d(x)>x^{\theta-\epsilon}$ for arbitrarily small positive ϵ and some arbitrarily large x, so that an X certainly exists.   This being so we may, for the purpose of a mere existence theorem, *assume* R.H., and my original proof did this.   For a numerical X it is natural to begin by still assuming R.H. Doing this, Dr. Skewes found [1] a new line of approach leading to

(1) $X=10^{10^{10^{34}}}$.

In this investigation it is possible to reduce the problem to a corresponding result about a function $\psi(x)$ associated with $\pi(x)$ [$\psi(x)$ is $\sum\limits_{n\leqslant x} \Lambda(n)$, where $\Lambda(n)$ is log p if n is a prime p or a power of p, and otherwise 0].   The ' corresponding result ' is

' $\delta(x)=\psi(x)-x-\tfrac{1}{2}x^{\frac{1}{2}}>0$ for some $x\leqslant X$ ' ;

[1] See *J.L.M.S* , 8 (1933), 277-283

H

if $\delta(x) > 0$ for some x then (roughly—I simplify details) $d(x) > 0$ for the same x. Next we have (roughly) an 'explicit formula' (R.H. or not)

$$(2) \qquad \frac{\delta(x)}{x^{\frac{1}{2}}} = -\tfrac{1}{2} - \Sigma \frac{x^{\beta-\frac{1}{2}}\sin \gamma\eta}{\gamma},$$

where $\beta+i\gamma$ is a typical complex zero of $\zeta(s)$ with positive γ, and we write $\eta = \log x$. Next, R.H. or not, a negligible error is committed by stopping the series in (2) when γ reaches x^3.

After these preliminaries we can consider the full problem of an X free of hypotheses, and the stages through which it went (this will involve a little repetition).

(i) Assume R.H. Then $\beta = \tfrac{1}{2}$ always, and it is a question of finding an $X = X_0$ such that

$$\sum_{\gamma < X^3} \frac{\sin \gamma\eta}{\gamma} > \tfrac{1}{2} \quad \text{for some } \eta \leqslant \log X.$$

The solution of this, which is a highly technical affair, is given in Dr. Skewes's *J.L.M.S.* paper. There is, as explained above, a final 'switch' from ψ to π (on well-established principles) and the X_0 arrived at is (1).

(ii) It is known that $\sum_{\gamma < T} 1/\gamma < A \log^2 T$ (it is actually of this order). If, instead of R.H., we assume slightly less, viz. that no zero with $\gamma < X_0{}^3$ has, say, $\beta \geqslant \tfrac{1}{2} + X_0^{-3} \log^{-3} X_0$, then

$$\sum_{\gamma < X_0{}^3} x^{\beta-\frac{1}{2}} \frac{\sin \gamma\eta}{\gamma} \text{ differs trivially over the range } x \leqslant X_0 \text{ from}$$

$$\sum_{\gamma \leqslant X_0{}^3} \frac{\sin \gamma\eta}{\gamma}, \text{ and we still have (after trivial readjustments)}$$

the conclusion   '$\delta(x) > 0$ for some $x \leqslant X_0$'.

(iii) It remains to prove the existence of a (new) X under the *negation* of the hypothesis in (ii). Now this negation is equivalent to the assertion of the existence of a $\beta_0 + i\gamma_0$ distant at least $b = X_0^{-3} \log^{-3} X_0$ to the right of $\Re s = \frac{1}{2}$, and with ordinate γ_0 not above X_0^3; i.e. we have a more or less *given* $\beta_0 + i\gamma_0$ with $\beta_0 - \frac{1}{2} \geqslant b$. Incidentally $\theta \geqslant \frac{1}{2} + b$ and there certainly *exists* an X. There is now a new surprise. With a $\beta_0 + i\gamma_0$ given as above we might reasonably expect the original θ-argument to provide an associated x with $\delta(x) > x^{\theta - \epsilon}$; alternatively, it is plausible that for *some* x the

series $\sum\limits_{\gamma < x^3} x^{\beta - \frac{1}{2}} \dfrac{\sin \gamma\eta}{\gamma}$ should exceed say 10^{-1} times the

value of its individual term $x^{\beta_0 - \frac{1}{2}} \dfrac{\sin \gamma_0\eta}{\gamma_0}$ (and with x

making the sine positive). Dr. Skewes, however, convinced me that the argument does not do this: it does not deal in individual terms, and the difficulty is that any term we select may be interfered with by other terms of its own order or greater. The difficulty is not at all trivial, and some further idea is called for. In the end I was able, in general outline, to supply this.

(iv) But the problem is still not done for. Dr. Skewes convinced me (this time against resistance) that in the absence of R.H. it is no longer possible to make the switch from ψ to π. This being so, it is necessary to carry through the work with the explicit formula for $\pi(x)$ instead of $\psi(x)$, with many attendant complications. This Dr. Skewes has done, and his result stands at present as $X = N_4(1 \cdot 46)$ [improved to $N_3(3)$].*

§ 15. The problem just considered prompts the question : could there be a case in which, while pure existence could be proved, no numerical X could be given *because any possible value of X was too large to be mentioned*? The mathematician's answer is ' no ', but we do thus return to the question, with which we began, of how large a number it is possible to mention. What we want is really a function $F(n)$ increasing as rapidly as possible ; what we finally substitute for n, whether 2, or u, or $N_u(u)$, makes no difference. (We must stop *somewhere* in constructing F, but one more step, say to $F(F(n))$, would overwhelm the difference in substitutions.)

We start with a strictly increasing positive $f_0(n)$. If we write $\psi^k(n)$ for the k-times iterated function $\psi(\psi(\ldots\psi(n)))$ we can define

$$f_1(n)=f_1(n, f_0)=f^{f^{f(n)}}(n) \text{ (to } f_0(n) \text{ indices, say),}$$

where for clarity we have suppressed the zero suffixes in the right-hand terms.

This defines an increase of suffix from 0 to 1 ; we suppose f_2 derived similarly from f_1 (in symbols $f_2(n)=f_1(n, f_1)$), and so on. We now take a hint from the notation of transfinite ordinals, and form

$$f_{f_{f_f(n)}}(n)$$

(to $f_{f(n)}(n)$ suffixes, say). We can now say : scrap the existing definitions, as scaffolding, and define *this* to be $f_1(n)$, and carry on as before. We can scrap again, and so on : here I decide to stop. Once we stop we may take $f_0(n)=n^2$, or $n+1$ (*what* we take does not matter provided only $f_0(n)>n$).

The reader will agree that the numbers mentioned are large : it is not possible to say *how* large ; all that can be said about them is that they are defined as they *are* defined. If it were desired to compare terms in two rival systems a considerable technique would have to be developed.

The Discovery of Neptune

Neptune was discovered in 1846 as a result of mathematical calculation, done independently and practically simultaneously by Adams and le Verrier. The full story abounds in unexpected twists, and is complicated by personal matters, some of them rather painful. There is a fascinating account in Professor W. M. Smart's *John Couch Adams and the Discovery of Neptune*, published by the Royal Astronomical Society, 1947. I am concerned only with limited parts of the field.

To refresh the reader's memory of what has been said from time to time about the discovery I will begin with some representative quotations. In *The Story of the Heavens* (1886) Sir Robert Ball has passages : ' the name of le Verrier rose to a pinnacle hardly surpassed in any age or country ' . . . ' profound meditations for many months ' . . . ' long and arduous labour guided by consummate mathematical artifice '. The author is not above a bit of popular appeal in this book—' if the ellipse has not the perfect simplicity of the circle, it has at least the charm of variety . . . an outline of perfect grace, and an association with ennobling conceptions '—but on Neptune he is speaking as a professional. An excellent modern book on the history of astronomy has, so late as 1938 : ' probably the most daring mathematical enterprise of the century . . . this amazing task, like which nothing had ever been attempted before '.

The immediate reaction was natural enough. Celestial Mechanics in general, and the theory of perturbations in particular, had developed into a very elaborate and highbrow subject ; the problem of explaining the misbehaviour of Uranus by a new planet was one of ' inverse ' theory, and the common feeling was that the problem was difficult up to or beyond the point of impossibility. One might speculate at some length on reasons for this opinion (one, perhaps was confusion between different meanings of the technica term ' insoluble ' [1]). When Adams and le Verrier provec the opinion wrong (and after all *any* mathematical proof is a debunking of sorts) there was still something to be said for the principle that difficulties are what they seem before the event, not after. Certainly no one would grudge them their resounding fame. (Nor grudge, at a lower level, the luck of a discovery which makes a more sensational impact than its actual difficulty strictly merits , in point of fact this luck never does happen to the second-rate.) If the discovery has had a very long run one must remember that there is a time-lag ; people cannot be always reconsidering opinions, and having said something once even the most intelligent tend to go on repeating it. The phrase was still in vogue that ' only 3 people understand Relativity ' at a time when Eddington was complaining that the trouble about Relativity as an examination subject in ' Part III was that it was such a soft option.

In what I am going to say I am far from imputing stupidity to people certainly less stupid than myself. My little *jeux d'esprit* are not going' to hurt anyone, and I refuse to be deterred by the fear of being thought disrespectful to great men. I have not been alone in a lurking suspicion that a much simpler approach might succeed. On the one hand, aim at the minimum needed to make observational discovery practicable ; specifically at the time t_0 of conjunction.[2] On the other, forget the high-brow and laborious perturbation theory, and try ' school mathematics '. (I admit to the human weakness of being spurred on by the mild piquancy success would have.) To begin with I found things oddly elusive (and incidentally committed some gross stupidities).

[1] Its attachment to the ' 3-body problem ' misleads people to-day
[2] The time at which NUS is a straight line (I shall use the abbreviations S, U, N).

In the end an absurdly simple line emerged : I can imagine its being called a dirty trick, nor would I deny that there is some truth in the accusation. The only way to make my case is to carry out the actual 'prediction' of t_0 from the observational data, with all the cards on the table (so that anyone can check against unconscious—or conscious— faking). I will also write so as to take as many amateurs as possible with me on the little adventure.

A planetary 'orbit' is an ellipse with the Sun S at a focus, and the radius vector SP sweeps out area at a constant rate (Kepler's second law). An orbit, given its plane, is defined by 4 elements, a, e, a, ϵ. The first 3 define the geometrical ellipse · a is the semi-major axis ; e the eccentricity ; a the longitude of perihelion, i.e. with the obvious polar co- ordinates r, θ, θ is the 'longitude' and $\theta = a$ when P is nearest S (at an end of the major axis). When we know a we know the 'mean angular velocity' n and the associated period $p = 2\pi/n$; n is in fact proportional to $a^{-\frac{3}{2}}$ (Kepler's third law)[1] ; further the constant rate of area sweeping is $\frac{1}{2}abn$,[2] and *twice* this rate is identical with the 'angular momentum'[3] (a.m. for short) ; this has the differential calculus formula $r^2\dot{\theta}$, and it also is of course constant. The 4th element, the 'epoch' ϵ, is needed to identify the origin of t ; the exact definition is that $\theta = a$ (perihelion) occurs at the t for which $nt + \epsilon = a$.

U's orbit has a period of 84 years, and an eccentricity e of about $\frac{1}{20}$. The effects of bodies other than S and N can be allowed for, after which we may suppose that U, S, and the eventual N are the only bodies in the system ; we may also suppose (all this is common form) that the move- ments are all in one plane. The values of θ (for U) at the various times t (we sometimes write $\theta(t)$ to emphasize that θ is 'at time t') may be regarded as the observational raw

---

[1] It does *not* depend on e.

[2] The total area of the ellipse is πab, and it is swept out in time p.

[3] Strictly speaking the a. m. should have the planet's mass as a factor : but U's mass is irrelevant and I omit it throughout.

material (though of course the actual raw observations are made from the Earth). The r's for the various t are indirect and are much less well determined.

The position in 1845 was that no exact elliptic orbit would fit the observed θ over the whole stretch 1780 to 1840.[1] The discrepancies are very small, mostly a few seconds of arc (with a sudden swoop of about $90''$, see Table I). The ratio m of N's mass to that of S (taken as 1) is actually about 1/19000 (the orders of magnitude fit since m radians is about $11''$).

In the absence of N the a.m. A is constant (as stated above —*alias* of Kepler's second law) ; *the actual N accelerates A at times earlier than t_0 and decelerates it at later times.* The graph of A against t therefore rises to a maximum at $t=t_0$, and my first idea was that this would identify t_0. So it would if all observations were without error (and the method would have the theoretical advantage of being unaffected by the eccentricities). But the value of A at time t depends on the r at time t, and the determinations of the A's are consequently too uncertain. Though the method fails it rises from the ashes in another form. For this a few more preliminaries are needed.

The numerical data Adams and le Verrier had to work on were not the observed θ's themselves, but the differences between the observed $\theta(t)$ and the $\theta_B(t)$ of an elliptic orbit calculated by Bouvard ; the ' discrepancy ' $\delta(t)$ (δ for short) is $\delta(t)=\theta(t)-\theta_B(t)$. [$\theta_B(t)$ depends on the ' elements ' of E_B, and these are subject to ' errors '. These errors are among the unknowns that the perturbation theory has to determine. our method does not mind what they are, as we shall see.] Table I gives the raw δ's (given in Adams's paper [2]), together with the values got by running a

---

[1] Observations after 1840 were not immediately available, and anyhow were not used Uranus was discovered in 1781. Lest the reader should be worried by small inconsistencies in my dates I mention that 1780 is ' used ', the extrapolation being a safe one.

[2] *Collected Works*, *I*, p. 11. These (and *not* the modifications he introduces, which are what appear in Smart) are what is relevant for us.

smooth curve. The treatment of the start of the sudden swoop down after the long flat stretch is a bit uncertain : I drew my curve and stuck to it (but faking would make no ultimate difference). The differences show up the order of the observational errors (which naturally improve with the years—something seems to have gone badly wrong in 1789) ; these are absolute, not relative (thus the probable absolute error in $\delta_1 - \delta_2$ is the same whether $\delta_1 - \delta_2$ is $0 \cdot 5''$ or $90''$). It is worth while to work to $0 \cdot 1''$ and to the number of decimal places used in what follows, even though the last place is doubtful.

TABLE I

Year	Observed δ	Smooth Curve	Year	Observed δ	Smooth Curve
1780	3 5	3 5	1813	22 0	22 8
1783	8 5	8 5	1816	22 9	22 5
1786	12 4	12 5	1819	20 7	22·0
1789	19 0	15 8	1822	21 0	21 0
1792	18 7	18 3	1825	18·2	18·1
1795	21·4	20 3	1828	10 8	10 3
1798	21 0	21 6	1831	− 4 0	− 4 0
1801	22 2	22 4	1834	−20·8	−20·8
1804	24 2	22 8	1837	−42 7	−42·5
1807	22 1	23 0	1840	−66 6	−66 6
1810	23 2	23 0	1843(e)	---	−94 0

The value for 1843 is an extrapolation ; results derived from it are labelled '(e)'.

An ' effect ' due to N is of ' order m ', in mathematical notation $O(m)$; if, for a particular quantity X, $\varDelta X$ denotes (calculated X)−(observed X), then any $\varDelta X$ is $O(m)$. The square of this (2nd order of infinitesimals) is extremely minute and everyone neglects it instinctively (if a watch loses 10 seconds a day you don't try to correct for the further loss over the lost 10 seconds—the cases are comparable). Next, an effect of N is what it would be if

U, and also N, moved in circles, *plus* a ' correction ' for the actual eccentricities of the orbits. U's eccentricity e $(\frac{1}{20})$ is unusually large and it would be reasonable to expect N's to be no larger (it is actually less than $\frac{1}{100}$). The e's distort the ' circular ' value of the effect by 5 per cent. (or say a maximum of 10 per cent.) , the ' distortion ' of the effect is $O(em)$, the effect itself being $O(m)$. I propose to ignore things of order $O(em)$ [1] : this is the first step in my argument. In particular, when we have something which is either some $\varDelta$, or m itself, multiplied by a *factor*, we can substitute first approximations (i.e. with $e=0$), or make convenient changes that are $O(e)$, in the *factor*.

Suppose now that E_1, E_2 are two (exact) elliptic orbits, yielding $\theta(t)$'s that differ by amounts of the kind we are concerned with, differing, that is, by $O(m)$.[2] It is now the case that *the differences satisfy the equation*

(1) $\theta_1 - \theta_2 = m(a+bt+c \cos nt+d \sin nt)+O(em),$

where a, b, c, d are constants depending on the two sets of elements of E_1, E_2, and (following our agreement about *factors* of m) n is any common approximation to the mean angular velocity. I will postpone the school mathematics proof of this.

Next, (i) let E^* be the ' instantaneous orbit at time t_0 ', that is to say the orbit that U would describe if N were annihilated at time t_0. note that E^* shares with t_0 the property of being ' unknown '. (ii) Let ϑ be the perturbation of the θ of U produced by N *since time t_0*.[3] Then if, at any time t, θ is (as usual) U's longitude, θ_B is the longitude in

---

[1] I should stress that there is no question of ignoring even high powers of e *unaccompanied by a factor* m (e^4 radians is about $1''$) The distortion in the value found for t_0 is, however, a sort of exception to this. But the effect of e's in distorting t_0 is unlikely to be worse than the separation they create between time of conjunction and time of closest approach. An easy calculation shows that this last time difference is at worst 0 8 years.

[2] The orbits may have ' Suns ' of masses differing by $O(m)$.

[3] We allow, of course, *negative* values of $t-t_0$ both in E^* and in ϑ.

the orbit E_B, and θ^* the longitude in the orbit E^*, we have $\backsim = \theta - \theta^*$, and so

(2) $$\delta(t) = \theta - \theta_B = (\theta^* - \theta_B) + \backsim.$$

Now everything in this has a factor m, and we may omit any stray $O(em)$'s. In particular, we may in calculating $\backsim$ drop *any* e terms. But this means that *we can calculate* $\backsim$ *as if both U's and N's orbits were circles.* When, however, the orbits are circles, $\backsim$ *has equal and opposite values at t's on equal and opposite sides of t_0*; in other words, *if we write $t = t_0 + \tau$, then*

(3) $$\backsim(t) = \Omega(\tau),$$

where $\Omega(\tau)$ is an odd [1] function of τ; i.e. $\Omega(-\tau) = -\Omega(\tau)$.

This, used in combination with (1) and (2), is the essential (and very simple) point of the argument. The difference $\theta^* - \theta_B$ is a special case of $\theta_1 - \theta_2$ in (1). Write $t = t_0 + \tau$ in (1) and combine this with (2) and (3); this gives, ignoring $O(em)$'s,

$$\delta(t_0 + \tau) = m\{a + bt_0 + b\tau + c\,\cos(nt_0 + n\tau) + d\,\sin(nt_0 + n\tau)\} + \Omega(\tau).$$

Expanding the cos and sin of sums and rearranging we have (with new constants, whose values vary with t_0 but do not concern us)

$$\delta(t_0 + \tau) = A - B(1 - \cos n\tau) + \{C\tau + D\,\sin n\tau + \Omega(\tau)\}.$$

The curly bracket is an odd function of τ. Hence if we combine equal and opposite τ and construct $\delta^*(\tau)$ and $\rho(\tau)$ to satisfy

$$\delta^*(\tau) = -\tfrac{1}{2}\{\delta(t_0 + \tau) + \delta(t_0 - \tau) - 2\delta(t_0)\}, \quad \rho(\tau) = \delta^*(\tau)/(1 - \cos n\tau),$$

we have $\delta^*(\tau) = B(1 - \cos n\tau)$, and so $\rho(\tau) = B$ for all τ. *If, then, we are using the right t_0, the ratio $\rho(\tau)$ must come out constant :*

---

[1] 'Ω' is a deputy for 'O' (initial of 'odd'), which is otherwise engaged.

The italicized statement in the text is true 'by symmetry': alternatively, *reverse* the motions from time t_0. (The argument covers also the 'perturbation of the *Sun*', which is not so completely negligible as might be supposed.)

this is our method for identifying t_0. The actual value of t_0 to the nearest year is 1822.

Table II, in which the unit of time is 1 year (and the n of $\cos n\tau$ is $2\pi/84$), shows the results of trying various t_0 (the century is omitted from the dates). The last place of decimals for the $\rho(\tau)$ is not reliable, but of course gets better as the size of the entry $2\delta^*(\tau)$ increases : I give the numbers as they came, and they speak for themselves. $\tau=6$ is included, though the proportionate error in δ^* is then considerable.[1] For $t_0=13$ ρ goes on to 34·8 at $\tau=27$; for $t_0=16$ it goes to 38·2 at $\tau=24$. Once the data—the smooth curve values—were assembled the calculations took a mere hour or so with a slide-rule. The date 1822·4 seems about the ' best ' t_0.

We need fairly large τ for $\delta^*(\tau)$ to have enough significant figures, and further to provide a range showing up whether $\rho(\tau)$ is constant or not. And we need room to manoeuvre round the final t_0. So the method depends on the ' luck ' that 1822 falls comfortably inside the period of observation 1780-1840. But *some* luck was needed in any case.

It is an important point that the method is quite indifferent to how well E_B does its originally intended job, and *we do not need to know (and I don't know) its elements* , it is enough to know the ' discrepancy ' with *some*, ' unknown ', orbit (not *too* bad of course). On the other hand the method ostentatiously says nothing at all about the mass or distance of N. I will add something on this. With e-terms ignored $\Im(\tau)/m$ can be calculated *exactly* for any given value of $\lambda=a/a_1$ (ratio of the a's of U and N).[2] The idea would be to try different λ's, each λ to give a best fitting m, and to take the best fitting *pair* λ, m. This fails, because the greater part

---

[1] And the values for $\tau=6$ at $t_0=22$, 22·4 are more uncertain than usual because of a crisis in the smooth curve.

[2] From two second order differential equations. The formula involves ' quadratures ', but in numerical calculation integration is quicker than multiplication. It would be comparatively easy to make a double entry table for $\Im(\tau, \lambda)/m$.

TABLE II

τ	$t_0=13$		$t_0=16$		$t_0=19$		$t_0=22$		$t_0=22.4$		$t_0=25$		$t_0=28$	
	$2\delta^*(\tau)$	$\rho(\tau)$	$2\delta^*(\tau)$	$\rho(\tau)$	$2\delta^*(\tau)$	$\rho(\tau)$	$2\delta^*(\tau)$	$\rho(\tau)$	$2\delta^*(\tau)$	$\rho(\tau)$	$2\delta^*(\tau)$	$\rho(\tau)$	$2\delta^*(\tau)$	$\rho(\tau)$
6	0·6	3·0	1·0	5·1	3·6	18·3	9·2	47·0	10·6	53·8	18·2	92·5	20·4	103
9	1·8	4·1	3·9	9·0	10·7	24·6	23·2	53·3	25·0	57·6	34·5	79·3	41·1	9·4
12	5·3	7·2	11·9	15·8	25·0	33·2	39·8	53·0	42·2	56·1	55·9	74·4	64·7	86
15	13·7	12·1	26·6	23·5	42·0	37·1	61·5	54·4	64·0	56·5	79·8	70·5	91(e)	80·6(e)
18	29·3	18·8	44·2	28·4	64·1	41·2	85·8	55·2	88·6	57·0	106(e)	68·3(e)	—	—
21	48·3	24·1	67·2	36·6	89·0	45·5	113(e)	56·5(e)	116(e)	58·0(e)	—	—	—	—

of ϑ is of the form $b'(n\tau - \sin n\tau)$, and b' is smothered by the a, b, c, d of $\theta^* - \theta_B$, which depend on the unknown elements of E_B (ϑ is smothered by the ' unknown ' $\theta^* - \theta_B$). If we *knew* these elements (or equivalently the raw θ) we might be able to go on. They could be recovered from the Paris Observatory archives ; but this article is a last moment addition to the book, I do not feel that I am on full professional duty, and in any case we should be losing the light-hearted note of our adventure.

The time t_0 once known, it would be necessary to guess a value for N's distance a_1 ; N's period is then $84(a_1/a)^{\frac{3}{2}}$ years, and we could ' predict ' N's place in 1846. The obvious first guess in 1846 was $a_1/a = 2$, following Bode's empirical law, to which N is maliciously the first exception, the true value being 1·58. Adams and le Verrier started with 2 (Adams coming down to 1·942 for a second round). Since from our standpoint [1] too large an a_1 has disproportionately bad results as against one too small, it would be reasonable to try 1·8. This would give a prediction (for 1846) about $10°$ out, but the sweep needed would be wholly practicable.

Le Verrier was less than $1°$ out (Adams between $2°$ and $3°$) ; ' they pointed the telescope and saw the planet '. This very close, and double, prediction is a curiosity. All the observations from 1780 to 1840 were used, and on an equal footing, and the theory purported to say where N was over this whole stretch. With a wrong a_1 they could be right at 1840 only by being wrong at 1780. With Adams's $a_1 = 1·94a$ N's period (which depends on a_1 only) would be 227 years ; he would have been wrong by $30°$ for 1780 if the orbit were circular, and so the angular velocity uniform. But faced with a wrong a_1 the method responded gallantly by putting up a large eccentricity ($\frac{1}{8}$), and assigning perihelion to the place of conjunction. The combination makes

---

[1] Perturbation theory calculations have necessarily to *begin* by guessing an a_1 ; our guess need only be at the end.

the effective distance from S over the critical stretch more like $1.7\ a_1$, and the resulting error at 1780 (the worst one) was only 18°. (A mass 2·8 times too large was a more obvious adjustment.)

In much more recent times small discrepancies for N and U (U's being in fact the more manageable ones) were analysed for a trans-Neptunian planet, and the planet Pluto was found in 1930 near the predicted place. This was a complete fluke : Pluto has a mass probably no more than $\frac{1}{10}$ of the Earth's ; any effects it could have on N and U would be hopelessly swamped by the observational errors.

It remains for me to give the (school mathematics) proof of (1) above. Call $e_1 - e_2\ \Delta e$, and so on. I said above that *all Δ's were $O(m)$* : this is not quite true, though my deception has been in the reader's best interests, and will not have led him astray.[1] It is true, and common sense, for Δa, Δe, Δn, and $\Delta\epsilon$. But the ' effect ' of a given Δa vanishes when $e=0$, and is proportional to e. *So it is $e\Delta a$, not Δa, that is comparable with the other Δ's and so $O(m)$.*[2]

We start from two well-known formulae. The first is geometrical ; the polar equation of the ellipse of the orbit is

$$(4) \qquad r=a(1-e^2)\ (1+e\cos(\theta-a))^{-1}.$$

The second is dynamical ; the equation of angular momentum (Kepler's second law) is

$$(5) \qquad r^2\frac{d\theta}{dt}=na^2(1-e^2)^{\frac{1}{2}}.$$

So, using dots for time differentiations,

$$(6) \qquad \dot\theta=n(1-e^2)^{-\frac{3}{2}}\ [1-2e\cos\ (\theta-a)+3e^2\cos^2\ (\theta-a)+\ \cdots].$$

---

[1] ' Wen Gott betrugt is wohl betrogen '

[2] This twist makes the ' obvious ' approach of using the well known expansion

$$\theta=nt+\epsilon+2e\sin\ (nt+\epsilon-a)+\tfrac{5}{4}\ e^2\sin\ 2(nt+\epsilon-a)+\ \cdots$$

slightly tricky , we should have to keep the term in e^2. The line taken in the text side-steps this.

The first approximation (with $e=0$) is $\theta=nt+\epsilon$. We take suffixes 1 and 2 in (6) and operate with $\varDelta$, remembering that we may take first approximations in any *factor* of an m.

In estimating $\varDelta\dot\theta$ we may, with error $O(em)$, ignore the factor $(1-e^2)^{-\frac{3}{2}}$ in (6), since it is itself $(1+O(e^2))$, and its $\varDelta$ is $O(e\varDelta e)=O(em)$. We have, therefore, with error $O(em)$,

$$\varDelta\dot\theta=\varDelta\{n[\ \ ]\}=[\ \ ]\varDelta n+n\varDelta[\ \ ].$$

The 1st term is $\varDelta n+O(em)$. The 2nd is

$$n[\varDelta e\{-2\cos(\theta-a)+O(e)\}+\varDelta(\theta-a)\{2e\sin(\theta-a)+O(e^2)\}],$$

and we may drop the θ in $\varDelta(\theta-a)$ on account of the factor $O(e)$. Summing up, we obtain

$$\varDelta\dot\theta=m(A+B\cos(\theta-a)+C\sin(\theta-a))+O(em),$$

where $mA=\varDelta n$, $mB=-2n\varDelta e$, $mC=-2n(e\varDelta a)$. Substituting the first approximation $\theta=nt+\epsilon$ in the right hand side, we have

$$\varDelta\dot\theta=m(A+B\cos(nt+\epsilon-a)+C\sin(nt+\epsilon-a))+O(em),$$

and integration then gives

$$\varDelta\theta=\varDelta\epsilon+m[At+(B/n)\sin(nt+\epsilon-a)$$
$$-(C/n)\cos(nt+\epsilon-a)]+O(em),$$

which, after expanding the sin and cos and rearranging, is of the desired form (1).[1]

---

[1] We have treated $\varDelta n$ and $\varDelta a$ as independent (the latter happens not to occur in the final formula for $\varDelta\theta$). this amounts to allowing different masses to the two 'Suns'. The point is relevant to certain subtleties, into which I will not enter.

The Adams–Airy Affair

Synopsis.[1] Adams called at the Royal Observatory on
Oct. 21, 1845, failed to see Airy, and left a note with a
short statement of his predictions about N. Airy's letter
of reply (Nov. 5) contained a question ' whether the errors
of the radius vector would be explained by the same theory
that explained the errors of longitude '. Adams did not
reply. The observational search did not begin till July 29,
1846, when Challis (in Cambridge) embarked on a comprehensive programme of sweeping (unfortunately much too
comprehensive) that continued to the end of September.
Le Verrier sent his predictions to the Berlin Observatory,
where Galle (aided by a recently published star map) found
N on Sept. 23, the day le Verrier's letter arrived.

What I have to say centres round these ' r-corrections '.
Adams started with a firm belief that the cause of U's
misbehaviour was an unknown planet, and a sure insight
into how to carry through the mathematics ; he was fully
concentrated on the job—' on duty '. Airy, not on duty,
thought, not at all unreasonably in 1845, that there might
be all sorts of other possibilities in an obscure field, and was
sceptical about a new planet. (And probably with a background, based on past analogies, that perturbation methods
would call for observational material over several revolu-
tions—many hundreds of years.) He did, however, raise
the question about r-corrections, and this unfortunately
became a pet idea. (Airy, in an ' explanation ' at the
R.A.S. meeting, Nov. 13, 1846 : ' I therefore considered that
the trial, whether the error of the radius vector would be
explained by the same theory which explained the error of
longitude, would be truly an *experimentum crucis*. And I

---

[1] The full story occupies the greater part of Smart's pp. 19-43.

I

waited with much anxiety for Mr. Adams's answer to my query. Had it been in the affirmative, I should have at once exerted all the influence etc '.) Adams (who said no word from first to last that failed in courtesy or generosity) did in fact not answer. His private reason [1] was that he thought the question trivial. What he says to Airy (in reply, Nov. 18, to the quotation above), omitting tactful apologies, is as follows. 'For several years past the observed place of Uranus has been falling more and more behind its tabular place. In other words the real angular motion of Uranus is considerably *slower* than that given by the tables. This appeared to me to show clearly that the tabular radius vector would be considerably increased by any theory which represents the motion in longitude, for the variation in the second member of the equation

$$r^2 \frac{d\theta}{dt} = \sqrt{(\mu a(1-e^2))}$$

is very small.[2] Accordingly I found that if I simply corrected the elliptic elements so as to satisfy the modern observations as nearly as possible, without taking into account any additional perturbations, the corresponding increase in the radius vector would not be very different from that given by my actual theory'. (The rest is irrelevant to the matters at issue.)

I find this (like so much written up to say 80 years ago [3]) very far from a model of lucidity ; but the essential point, that the a.m. varies very little, could not be clearer. And then 'constancy' of the a.m. does establish a simple linkage between the θ-errors and the r-errors. Challis (after the discovery) agrees : 'It is quite impossible that

---

[1] Given in a conversation with Glaisher in 1883.

[2] [$r^2 \frac{d\theta}{dt}$ is the angular momentum (a.m. for short).   J.E.L.]

[3] A man had to be of 'Fellowship standard' to read a paper with understanding ; to-day a marginal Ph D. candidate can *read* anything.

[U's] longitude could be corrected during a period of at least 130 years independently of the correction of the radius vector . . . '. Adams is finally confirmed in his view by the actual numerical calculations ; the variation of (the appropriate multiple of) the a.m. contributes only a small part to the θ-effects.

The first thing to note is that Airy and Adams are partly at cross-purposes. Airy's background is : I doubt the explanation by a planet, but would take it up if it explained the r's as well as the θ's. Adams's is : a planet is the explanation, and if it is determined to fit the θ's it can't help (on account of the ' linkage ') fitting the r's too. Adams was I think at fault in not seeing and allowing for this ; he did later admit that not giving a reasoned answer at once amounted to a lapse on his part. It is probably relevant that besides being the fine mathematician he was Adams happened also to be very much the ' Senior Wrangler type ' (an extreme form, on its own ground, of the bright young man) ; knowledge and ideas in pigeon holes available at any moment ; effortlessly on duty. Older people, off duty whenever possible, and with pigeon holes mislaid, can seem slow and stupid.[1] Always answer the ' trivial ' questions of your elders (and it is just possible even for a bright young man to be overlooking something).

I have been keeping up my sleeve the fact that on the crucial theoretical point about the a.m. Adams was dead wrong. The variation in the a.m. is proportionately of the

---

[1] No one who does not meet eminent people off duty would credit what they are capable of saying I recall two conversations at the Trinity High Table. One of the most eminent of biologists was asked whether two sons, one from each of two marriages, of identical twin brothers to identical twin sisters, would be identical, he replied ' yes ', and was corrected by a philosopher whose pigeon holes are always in unusually good working order In the other Rutherford, Fowler, at least one other physicist, and myself got into a hopeless muddle between the alleged ' penny and feather in a vacuum ' experiment and the fact that viscosity is independent of density. Was the experiment a bluff ? Rutherford said apologetically that he *thought* he had seen it done as a boy. The muddle continued until after dinner we were put out of our misery by an engineer.

same order as the θ-error. This is obvious from the point of view of school mathematics (take 'moments' about S : N pulls hard at the a.m.).[1] Adams's point of view was consistently perturbation theory, but even so, and granted that even a Senior Wrangler type can make a slip, it is an odd slip to make.[2] The numerical confirmation is a last touch of comedy. In 'small contribution' 'small' means small in the sense that 15 per cent. is small, not 'very' small (Adams's word). But in any case this 'smallness' is an accident of the numerical constants ; e.g. it does not happen for a 'distant' N.

Postscript on Celestial Mechanics

I will wind this up by debunking a recent piece of work of my own, which has as a consequence that *a gravitating system of bodies* (a generalization of the Solar System) *can never make a capture, even of a speck* (or, reversely, suffer a loss).[3] This is 'sensational' (I have not met a mathematician who does not raise his eyebrows), and contrary to some general beliefs. I should add : (i) it is not that the speck promptly goes out again ; it may be retained for any number of billion years. And there are *limiting* cases in which the capture is permanent ; but these are to be rejected as being infinitely rare, just as we reject a permanent state of unstable equilibrium (a pin on its point). These infinitely rare happenings, however, show that the statement cannot be trivial. (ii) The proof in no way shows that it is the speck that goes out, it might be Jupiter.

The result is a consequence of the following one : *suppose a system has been contained within a fixed sphere S for all negative time, then (unless it is one of an infinitely rare set)*

[1] The full analysis of the circular case of course confirms this.

[2] $1-e^2$ has 'small variation', but what makes him think that a has ?

[3] The bodies are idealized to be point-masses, to avoid bumps arising from finite size, and subject to Newton's inverse square law of gravitation (this is probably not essential). A number of inquiries have failed to disclose any previous statement of the result.

t will be so contained for all positive time. Similarly with positive and negative times reversed. (To see that the former result *is* a consequence, observe that any *genuine* capture, or escape, must involve a difference between past and future time that is ruled out.)

Take the theorem in its (slightly more convenient) reverse form : the ideas for proving it are as follows. A system ' is associated with a representative point (r.p. for short), P say, of a ' phase space ', embodying the ' initial conditions ' at a fixed time t_0, say $t_0 = 0$.[1] Now take the set ' V (in the $6n$-space) of *all* points P representing systems that (in the astronomical space) stay in the sphere S for all positive time. The ' system ' P has a new r.p., P' (co-ordinates $x, \ldots, \dot{x}, \ldots$), at time (say) $t = 1$, and to the set V of P's there corresponds a set V' of P's. A well-known theorem, which we will take for granted, says that [because the differential equations for the system are ' conservative '] the ($6n$-dimensional) volumes of V and V' are equal.[2]

Next, consider V' as in the *same* $6n$-space as V. For a r.p. P to belong to V it has to satisfy a certain entrance examination, namely that all its bodies should stay in S in the *future* of the system. Now any P' of V' is derived from some P of V, P's ' future ' starts time 1 later than P's, and its bodies stay in S ; P' *satisfies the entrance examination.* So : *the set V' is contained in V.* But the volumes of V' and V are equal. The two things together clearly require the sets V' and V to be *identical* [as *wholes* ; the *collection* of P's is the same as the collection of P's]. So *a point Q of V is some point or other of V, R say.*

Now start with a point Q of V, and take the corresponding r.p. at time $t = -1$ (time 1 into the past). Q is an R of V', and is therefore ' derived ' (i.e. as P' is ' derived ' from P)

---

[1] If there are $n+1$ bodies the phase space has $6n$ dimensions, the coordinates ' being the (astronomical) space coordinates x_0, y_0, z_0 and the corresponding velocities $\dot{x}_0$, $\dot{y}_0$, $\dot{z}_0$ of n of the bodies at time t_0.

[2] *Any* set V has the same volume at all t. For the professional there is 1-line proof (if you can call Jacobian determinants a line).

from some T of V. This T *is* the r.p. of P at $t=-1$. So : *the r.p. at $t=-1$ of a P of V is itself in V.* Now this repeats *indefinitely* into the past : if P is in V at $t=0$ the corresponding r.p. is in V at times [of the form $t=-m$] going back into the infinite past. This means that its bodies stay in S in the *whole* of the infinite past, and we have arrived.

This argument is an astonishing example of the power of general reasoning. If the ideas in it were my own I should indeed have done something ; but they are at least 60 years old. What happened to *me* was this. I had been lecturing for some time on differential equations of a kind for which the volume corresponding to V *decreases* with increasing t. The ' constant volume theorem ' (which in my innocence I had learned only recently) came to mind, and I switched over to the Celestial Mechanics equations by way of a change. During a stroll after the lecture the argument I have given flashed through my mind (literally in a matter of seconds). My first feeling was that I could not publish a thing which had so little originality. But finding myself hopelessly behindhand with a promised contribution to a *Festschrift* I began considering details. It is the way people think who ever think of anything new at all, but taken strictly the argument contains some lies (3 to be exact). To straighten these out is a job any competent analyst could do, but it puts up a colourable appearance of backbone. So the *trouvaille* was written up [1] : brilliant ideas, not mine, *plus* a routine job.

---

[1] The paper is in : *Communications du séminaire mathématique de l'Université de Lund, tome supplémentaire (1952), dédié à Marcel Riesz.* There is a tail-piece to show that the initial assumption that no body has actually *zero* mass can be dispensed with. This minute addition is not trivial ; indeed it took a fortnight's damned hard work (But though the essential idea takes pages to state it came to me on a walk, and this time literally in a *fraction* of a second.)

'Lion and Man'

A lion and a man in a closed arena have equal maximum speeds. What tactics should the lion employ to be sure of his meal ? ' [1]

It was said that the ' weighing-pennies ' problem wasted 10,000 scientist-hours of war-work, and that there was a proposal to drop it over Germany. This one,[2] though 25 years old, has recently swept the country ; but most of us were teased no more than enough to appreciate a happy idea before arriving at the answer, ' L keeps on the radius OM '.

If L is off OM the asymmetry helps M. So L keeps on OM, M acts to conform, and irregularity on his part helps L. Let us then simplify to make M run in a circle C of radius a with angular velocity ω. Then L (keeping to the radius) runs in a circle touching C,[3] at P, say, and M is caught in time less than π/ω. This follows easily from the equations of motion of L, namely $\dot{\theta}=\omega$, $\dot{r}^2+r^2\omega^2=a^2\omega^2$. It is, however, instructive to analyse the motion near P. For this

$$\dot{r}\geqslant(a-r)^{\frac{1}{2}}/K, \quad \text{and} \quad t< \text{const.} + K\!\int(a-r)^{-\frac{1}{2}}dr.$$

The integral converges (as $r\to a$) with plenty to spare— plenty, one would guess, to cover the use of the simplifying hypothesis. ⋆ The professional will easily verify that when M spirals outwards to a circle, and, with obvious notation (ω varying), we write $x=r_{\text{M}}-r_{\text{L}}$, we have $-\dot{x}\geqslant(\omega^2 r_{\text{L}})(x/\dot{r}_{\text{L}})=X$, where $X/x\to\infty$. Then $t< \text{const.} + \int_x^{-1} X\,dx$, and in this the integral increases more slowly than $\int_x^{-1} x\,dx$: it is a generally safe guess in such a case that the integral *converges*.⋆

All this notwithstanding, the ' answer ' is wrong, and M can escape capture, (no matter what L does).[4] This has just

---

[1] 'The curve of pursuit' (L running always straight at M) takes an infinite time, so the wording has its point

[2] Invented by R. Rado (unpublished)

[3] The case when L starts at O is particularly obvious, on geometrical grounds.

[4] I used the comma in l. 9, p. 135 to mislead ; it does not actually cheat.

been discovered by Professor A. S. Besicovitch; here is the first (and only) version in print.

I begin with the case in which L does keep on OM ; very easy to follow, this has all the essentials in it (and anyhow shows that the 'answer' is wrong). Starting from M's position M_0 at $t=0$ there is a polygonal path $M_0M_1M_2 \ldots$ with the properties · (i) M_nM_{n+1} is perpendicular to OM_n, (ii) the total length is infinite, (iii) the path stays inside a circle round O inside the arena. In fact, if $l_n = M_{n-1}M_n$ we have $OM_n^2 = OM_o^2 + \sum_{}^{n} l_m^2$, and all is secured if we take $l_n = cn^{-\frac{1}{2}}$, with a suitable c. Let M run along this path (L keeping, as agreed, on OM). Since M_0M_1 is perpendicular to L_0M_0, L does not catch M while M is on M_0M_1. Since L_1 is on OM_1, M_1M_2 is perpendicular to L_1M_1, and L does not catch M while M is on M_1M_2. This continues for each consecutive M_nM_{n+1}, and for an infinite time since the total length is infinite.

⋆ I add a sketch, which the professional can easily complete, of the astonishingly concise proof for the quite general case. Given M_0 and L_0, M *selects* a suitable O (to secure that the boundary does not interfere with what follows), and constructs the polygon $M_0M_1M_2 \ldots$ described above, but runs along another one, $M_0M_1'M_2' \ldots$, associated with it, but depending on what L does. M_0M_1' is drawn perpendicular to L_0M_0, N_0 is the foot of the perpendicular from O on M_0M_1', and M_1' is taken beyond N_0 from M_0 so that $N_0M_1' = l_1 (= M_0M_1)$. If L is at L_1 when M is at M_1', $M_1'M_2'$ is drawn perpendicular to L_1M_1', and M_2' taken on it so that $N_1M_2' = l_2$; and so on. Clearly $OM_n'^2 - OM_{n-1}'^2 \leqslant l_n^2$, $OM_n'^2 \leqslant OM_n^2$, and the new polygon is inside the same circle as the old one. Since $M_{n-1}'M_n' \geqslant l_n$ the new polygon has again infinite length. And as before L fails to catch M.⋆

Printed in Great Britain
by T. and A CONSTABLE LTD , Hopetoun Street,
Printers to the University of Edinburgh

CPSIA information can be obtained
at www.ICGtesting.com
Printed in the USA
BVHW040406271218
536340BV00003B/87/P

9 781376 177626